Dear Diary...

The secret feelings of a junior high girl

PAT BAKER

Tyndale House Publishers, Inc.
Wheaton, Illinois

Unless otherwise stated, Scripture quotations are
from *The Living Bible*, copyright © 1971 owned by
assignment by KNT Charitable Trust. All rights
reserved. Other Scripture quotations are from the
Holy Bible, King James Version (KJV); or the *Holy
Bible,* New International Version (NIV), copyright
© 1973, 1978, 1984 International Bible Society. Used
by permission of Zondervan Bible Publishers.

Library of Congress Catalog Card Number 89-51965
ISBN 0-8423-0536-X
Copyright © 1990 by Pat Baker
All rights reserved
Printed in the United States of America

96 95 94 93 92
8   7   6   5   4   3   2

To Lindey, a special young girl in my life

Dear Diary,

These people used to be in junior high. I don't want to ever forget that they helped me every time I asked them to while I was writing this book.

Pam, Dana, and Beth, who said it was OK to share some of their junior high secrets;

Pam, Dana, and Beth's dad, who survived their junior high years;

Sandy Asher, author and creative writing professor; Dr. Ron Kemp, Christian family counselor; Lynn Noyes, R.N.; Dr. William Donnell, M.D.;

Judy Kallenbach, newspaper editor;

Mary Fullerton, Jean Fullerton, school counselors; Evelyn Fullerton, school nurse; Addie Johnson and Judy Dutile, college professors in home economics and family relations; Ann Kitchin, college librarian;

Geri Moore, Robert Buffington, Linda Rice, Doug Potts, Marla Roberts, Jean Parsons, Kendall Ebersold — all teachers;

Sandy Jones, women's clothier;

Caroline Brown Raley and Sonya Strader, beauty consultants;

J.C.S., who let me use one of her beautiful poems;

The principals and teachers who gave permission for their students to fill out the questionnaires and who let me use class time to ask the girls and boys more questions;

The junior high girls and boys who wrote such honest answers on their questionnaires so that the kids who read this book would know they're normal!

Theo Clark, Doris Hooper, Mary Purcell, Twila Smith — special friends who prayed for me as I wrote this book;

The three beautiful junior high girls I got to know better while I was writing this book: Tiffany, Shonda, and Amy;

And the three people from Tyndale House Publishers who encouraged me and believed I could write about the secret feelings of junior high girls: Dr. Wendell Hawley, Ken Petersen, and Karen Ball.

Love, Pat

CONTENTS

INTRODUCTION

Secrets

On a hot summer day in July, I crawled up into my attic to look for the diary I had kept when I was twelve years old.

I knew exactly what I was looking for. The outside of the diary looked like black alligator skin. The pages were edged in gold. On the front of the diary, printed in gold, were the words *One Year Diary*. The diary's most important feature was the brass lock that kept intruders out! I always locked my diary after I wrote in it. Then I found several places to hide the key. I would have died if anyone had read what I had written. I used abbreviations that only I would understand for certain words. Also I used initials for certain boys' names.

As I searched through several boxes, I unexpectedly found the diary one of my daughters had kept when she was twelve. I laid it down, deciding to ask her later if I could read it. After digging in several other places, I found my diary in an old suitcase. I could hardly wait to climb down the ladder and open the pages, to rediscover the forgotten secrets of my twelfth year.

Most of the diary was about one certain boy I'd liked in eighth grade. He had moved to town that year and he was the best-looking boy I had ever seen. I liked him until he moved away three years later. He never knew how much I liked him. All I could do was write about my feelings for him in my diary.

Later, after my daughter had read her diary, she told me I could read it. As I read, I compared what she had written with what I had written in my diary. I noticed we had written about many of the same subjects and feelings. We'd written about the boys we liked and about the girls we didn't like (because they liked the same boys we did). We'd written about our favorite — and not-so-favorite — teachers. We'd both used initials to disguise the boys we wrote about.

After I read both diaries, I began to wonder if all junior high girls have similar feelings. I decided to make up and mail questionnaires to junior high girls across the United States. On the questionnaire, I explained I was considering writing a book for junior high girls, and I needed their help. Then I listed questions concerning their feelings about themselves, boys, other girls, teachers, and parents. I asked the girls to answer the questions as honestly as they could.

The response was great! In a few weeks I had received back a huge stack of questionnaires. The girls' answers were very honest. Some girls wrote such honest answers that they put their questionnaires in one envelope, sealed it, then put *that* envelope inside another envelope and sealed it. A few of the girls even wrote personal notes at the end of their questionnaires. They told me to hurry and get the book written so they could read it and see if their feelings were normal. (You will find many of their comments in this book, but I've changed the names to protect their privacy.)

These weren't the only girls who helped me prepare to write this book. There were three other girls, girls I had lived with and had observed carefully as they went through their junior high years: my daughters, Pam, Dana, and Beth. I honestly hadn't realized how miserable my own daughters had been at times during their junior high years until one day a year after Beth graduated from high school. On that day, as we sat in front of a junior high school watching all the kids changing classes, Beth said, "No one should be junior high age!"

She told me about many of the unspoken feelings she had had during those years. Later, I asked Pam and Dana how they felt when they were that age. Both of them told me that some of the worst days of their lives had happened during their junior high years. They told me how self-conscious they had been about their bodies, especially when they didn't develop the way they'd pictured them developing. They confessed they had made all kinds of excuses not to use the public swimming pools because they couldn't find bathing suits that covered the parts of their bodies they didn't want anyone to see! Shopping for a bra that would fit had been total torture. They told me they had wanted so badly for certain boys to notice them, but it was usually the boys they couldn't stand who noticed them and wouldn't leave them alone! There had been days when all three of my girls felt no one liked or understood them.

Between my daughters' comments and the stack of questionnaires I received, I knew I had to write this book. When some mothers of junior high girls found out I was going to write this book, they told me to hurry and get it done so *they* could read it! They wanted to understand how their daughters were feeling and why.

Before I started writing, I read many books that had been written for girls in junior high. As I read, I noticed something very important was missing. From the answers the girls had written on their questionnaires, I had learned how important God was in their lives. But few of the books said anything about God and how he could fit in or help girls with what they were experiencing. So I decided to use special Words from the Scriptures to help you know how deeply God feels and cares about you—and how he *completely* understands all the changes and new feelings you're having. If nothing else, I hope these special Words from God will give you a clue as to how really special you are!

How Special Are You?

Has anyone stopped you at home, at school, or on the street and told you that the world's a better place because you're in it? Probably not, but it's true.

Maybe you're going through some incredible body changes now. You may be having new feelings about yourself and everyone else—feelings you never had until you hit junior high. As hard as it may be to believe, whatever you are feeling is OK. It's even normal! It's all a part of "graduating" from a girl to a woman. Your job is to do whatever it takes to understand, work with, and even *enjoy* all the changes going on!

After you read this book, I'd love to hear from you. Let me know if what you've read has helped you know how special and normal you are. You can write me in care of Tyndale House Publishers, Inc., 336 Gundersen Dr., P.O. Box 80, Wheaton, IL, 60189.

Whether you write me or not I want to be the first one to tell you: You *are* special!

Love,
Pat

ONE

Secret
Feelings
about
Yourself

> *Dear Diary,*
> *I'm in junior high school now! I thought it would be so*
> *wonderful. And it is. Sometimes. But it's scary too.*
> *Everything is changing. Me. My body. Mom says don't*
> *worry, I'm just becoming a woman . . . but sometimes it*
> *makes me wonder what's going to happen next. I can't*
> *believe I'm changing so fast! I'm not too sure I like it.*
> *What's wrong with me?*
>
> *Lindey*

I often wonder why someone didn't explain to me what
would happen to my body when I turned twelve, and how I
would feel about myself. Why didn't some wise woman sit
down with me and tell me that the changes were normal?
Or that I needed to love and accept myself while all of these
body changes were going on? Or that accepting myself has
everything to do with understanding the special plan God
had for me when he designed me?

Since I didn't know how all these changes would affect
the way I felt about myself, I had a lot of trouble accepting

the first change that came. It started in the eighth grade—I started growing very tall. I really thought the rest of my body wasn't developing as fast as some of the other girls'. So I was self-conscious about my underdeveloped body.

I panicked the first time I saw the room where I would dress for P.E. I had figured the room would have private stalls where each girl could undress and shower. Wrong! It was one huge bare room with *public* showers and a few benches. I had to come up with a quick plan because I didn't want other girls to see my nude, flat body. I learned to take record-breaking showers while hiding behind my big towel. The best days were when I got excused from taking P.E. because I had my period. (That excuse doesn't work now, but I was sure glad they let *us* use it!)

At the same time my body started changing, I began changing my opinion about boys. They started to look more interesting than they had in elementary school. Being self-conscious about my height, I just knew there would never be a boy taller than me, which meant no boy would *ever* ask me out on a date.

It really hurt when certain guys made remarks about my height. I talked to my mother about it and she told me she had been the tallest girl in her class, too. I asked her if guys had ever made remarks about her height. She told me how she had learned to handle it. She said that once when a boy asked her, "How's the weather up there?" she just spit on him and said, "It's raining!" That ended his dumb remarks about her height!

Her story made me feel a little better, but I still wanted to look like the other girls in my class. What I needed was someone to tell me that the feelings I was having about myself were normal. That may be what you need to hear, too. To understand what normal is or isn't, check out this science fiction scene:

You arrive at school and go to your locker. The hall is full of kids rushing to get to their first-hour class. Every girl you see has brown, curly hair and brown eyes. They are the same height and weight. Their arms, feet, skin, ears, and noses are all alike.

You say hi to several of your friends. They say hi back—and your voices are identical. Then you notice the boys. They're all the same height, about 5'5", and the same weight. They all have blond hair, blue eyes, and freckles. Their voices are identical, too.

Boring? You bet! Like pizza without any toppings or hamburgers without fries. God never planned for us to look alike, or for our bodies to develop at the same pace. He planned for each one of us to be an original. Here's how God put his plan into action: "[God] made all the delicate, inner parts of [your] body and knit them together in [your] mother's womb. . . . [He was] there while [you were] being formed in utter seclusion" (Psalm 139:13, 15).

Your special design was put into production when one sperm out of millions, all the size of a pinpoint and produced by your dad, united with an egg the size of a pinhead, produced by your mom. Then, the second after the sperm and egg made contact . . . talk about body changes! No one but God could have come up with such an original plan to create a human being.

In that split second when the sperm and egg united, you instantly became a tiny, living, complicated organism. Your cells began to multiply like crazy. God saw what was going on and began to direct the way you were formed. He was the only one who knew what you would look like when you were born. He stayed with you and your mom all those months to make sure your design was exactly the way he planned it.

17

When you reached "Destination: World," you looked different from any other baby who had ever been born. Your birth was a once-in-a-lifetime event — a miracle. Your beautiful body has been changing since day one. Then, sometime during your elementary school years, your body took some time off from doing anything but growing a little taller. When it finally got back into full production, your shape and your facial features started changing. You probably wondered what was happening and if these changes were normal.

You have two choices when your body starts to change: You can enjoy the changes or you can feel miserable and self-conscious about them. Take the first choice so you can explore and enjoy the miracles that are taking place with your body!

> *"I used to think I was a 'dud,' but I look back at my pictures and I really didn't look so bad. When I look at myself now, I'm satisfied."* Sherry, 10th grade

In Psalm 139:16, God says that he scheduled each day of your life *before* you were born. "Each day" includes today, all your junior high years, and all the years after that. God scheduled this specific time in your life when your body and feelings would be making all kinds of changes.

Right now you're getting acquainted with a body that hasn't quite made it to the finish line, but the end result will be exactly the way God designed it. If you want your body to look differently from the way God designed it, check out these special Words: "Do [you] argue with [your] maker? Do [you] dispute with him who forms [you], saying, 'Stop, you're doing it wrong!' or . . . exclaim, 'How clumsy can you be!'? . . . [The] Creator, says: What right have you to question what I do? Who are you to command me concern-

ing the work of my hands? I have made the earth and created [you]" (Isaiah 45:9, 11-12).

How Girls Feel about Their Body Changes

"My looks are improving. I'm beginning to develop a figure
  but I wish it would develop quicker." Jenny, 8th grade

"I wish I was bigger on top." Ann, 7th grade

"I don't think my legs will ever fill out." Kerry, 8th grade

"When I was twelve, I was the shortest person in my class.
  (I still am.) At the time it bothered me, but it doesn't
  now." Julie, 9th grade

"I hated me at twelve. I'm OK now." Karen, 9th grade

"When I notice my body changing, I sometimes want to be
  a little girl again because I'm not used to the changes, but
  it's good in a way because it shows I'm growing and
  maturing." Laurie, 9th grade

"I didn't like my body when I started junior high and that
  held me back from being more outgoing. But now I don't
  feel that way. I've grown up and filled out better in a few
  places." Gloria, 10th grade

One of the First Changes: Breast Development

Just when I finally started accepting my height, my breasts
starting changing. I checked them out one afternoon and
noticed they were sore and slightly swollen. I wondered
how long it would be before I could wear a bra, but at the
same time I worried that someone would notice my breasts
changing and make a remark about it. I can relate to the girl
who wrote on her questionnaire that she wished her "top
was bigger." From start to finish, my breasts had a short
growing season. I found I could improve how I looked by
wearing certain clothing styles. (Check out the box,
"Choose the Right Clothes to Look Your Best.")

Many junior high girls feel they are either behind or ahead of schedule when they compare their development with their friends' development. Some girls are waiting to graduate from training bras and dream of the day they will fill a B-cup bra like some of their friends. The B-cup group often tries to convince the training-bra group that they'd rather have smaller breasts. The "trainees" are convinced the B-cup group looks older in their clothes and gets more attention from boys, but the B group hates it when guys get together and make embarrassing remarks to them about their breasts!

So there's really no middle ground with this newest body change. The girls with small breasts keep waiting for their breasts to change so their bodies won't look like they did in the fourth grade and so clerks will stop directing them to the children's section when they're shopping. The other group practices slumping and wears the kind of clothing that makes their breasts look smaller.

It's good that breast change is a steady, slow process. It would be a shock if you woke up one morning and saw your breasts had grown from start to finish during the night! Don't worry if it looks like your breasts are taking forever to develop. It takes time to shape up!

Choose the Right Clothes to Look Your Best

These ideas may help you feel more comfortable with your newly developed bustline:

• If your bustline is small, think "loose clothing." You'll feel and look great wearing lighter colors on your top half and darker colors on your bottom half.

• If you have a large bustline, wear dark colors on the top half and light colors on the bottom half. "V" necklines are OK as long as they aren't too low-cut. Wear collars open. Form vertical lines with necklaces, stitching, or vertical tucks to compliment your body. Small belts the same color as your skirts, dresses, and slacks are a plus to your outfits.

Another Change: Zit Attacks

Another change usually creeps in between the ages of twelve and fourteen. A chemical imbalance shows up and the oil glands get overstimulated. The results? A minor or major Zit Attack.

A zit attack shows up in pimples, blackheads, or whiteheads. When a pimple shows up some morning before school or after school, someone, probably the class comedian or even a good friend, will make some comment about it. "Did you know you have a pimple?" "Wow! I've never seen such a big pimple. Does it hurt?" "If it wasn't on the end of your nose, I probably wouldn't have noticed it."

Pimples always feel like they grow bigger and brighter when you're around girls who don't have pimples yet. Pimple-free girls can't seem to understand how one zit can make a person feel miserable.

As hard as some girls try to avoid it, they can't seem to stop full-scale pimple invasions. They often invent hairstyles that cover the zits, or use layers of makeup as camouflage. Then they may plan to (a) sit in the back row in their classes and act invisible, (b) find a dark corner and stand facing the wall during lunch hour, (c) stay ten feet away from everyone with 20/20 vision, or (d) pray for dark, cloudy days.

How Girls Feel about Their Complexion

"I have zits a lot. I'm talking major!" Jill, 9th grade

"I had a terrible complexion, or at least I thought I did. I went to a dermatologist and he helped me solve some of the problems." Debbie, 9th grade

"If my face breaks out, it's usually right before my period. I wash my face twice a day and don't use much makeup

21

except for special occasions." Jennifer, 10th grade
"I keep my face clean and take zinc. When my skin dries
out I use a little moisturizer." Carole, 8th grade

I never had a full-scale pimple attack, but I could count on one large zit attacking the same place on my chin every month. It showed up right on schedule, a day or two before my period. I dreaded going to school because I felt sure everyone would stare at my pimple. I used makeup to hide the redness, but it couldn't hide the bump. It was very painful. The biggest pain was being afraid that people would guess that I had my period because of the zit.

If you are struggling with complexion problems, don't give up! *No one* has ever gotten through life without a few zit skirmishes, and no fatalities from major zit attacks have ever been recorded in any medical journal. Remember, God gave you the perfect face for you. You can keep it beautiful by using proper skin care and cleansing methods. Here's a three-minute plan for keeping your face beautiful!

First and foremost, you must keep your face 99.9 percent clean. Use a transparent soap bar with glycerin in it. Using regular hand soap can strip too much oil out of your skin, which would only make the oil glands work triple time.

To clean your face properly:

1. Wash your hands before they ever touch your face. You'll do this if you take thirty seconds to remember everything your hands have touched in twenty-four hours.

2. Wet your face with lukewarm water.

3. Use your fingertips to gently massage the soap into your skin for sixty to ninety seconds. Get into the creases around your nose and chin, and get as close to your hairline as possible. These are primary targets for acne attacks.

4. Rinse your face with lukewarm water until you can't feel any more soap.

5. Splash your face with cool water to close your pores.
6. Use a soft towel to pat (don't rub) your face dry.

Extra Facial Care

1. Twice a week, stimulate your skin for a healthier complexion. With gentle, circular motions, rub your forehead, cheeks, and chin with a clean, wet, lukewarm terry washcloth. This helps get rid of dry cells, opens blocked pores, and reduces the chance of getting blackheads. It also increases blood circulation, which is great for a beautiful complexion.

2. A facial steam bath is fun to do with a friend. It's another way to open up your pores. Heat water in a large pan until it starts to steam. With help from your friend or from one of your parents, carefully remove the water from the stove and place it on the table. Hold your faces comfortably above the water. Cover your heads and the pan with a large, clean towel. This will catch the steam. Stay under the towel until your faces perspire and feel warm. Pat dry.

3. Eating certain foods can help keep your face beautiful. Raw vegetables, green leafy vegetables, orange vegetables, and whole grain breads are best. Nutritionists say that oatmeal, pork, and peanuts are good for healthy skin, especially around your mouth, nose, and eyes. Since constipation can cause complexion problems, eat foods with Vitamin C (oranges, for example) to prevent it.

A Strange Change: New Hair Locations

Another body change you will experience during your junior high years is the appearance of fine new hair under your arms, on your legs, and around your genital area. It won't be long until you have the urge (if you haven't had it already) to shave your legs.

I wanted to start shaving my legs when I was in the eighth grade. Several of my friends had started shaving and their legs looked great. When I asked my mother if I could shave my legs she said, "You know once you start you can never stop!" I wanted to do it so badly that doing it *forever* didn't discourage me.

I went into the bathroom, put lots of soap lather on my legs, and shaved very slowly. I rinsed, dried, and put lotion on my legs. I can still feel the sensation of my smooth legs against my skirt. I loved it!

Some girls shave their legs in secret and then suddenly appear before their surprised parents with hairless, freshly razor-scraped legs. This isn't the best way to develop friendly family relations, but most parents continue to love their kids whether they decide to keep the leg hairs attached or to go hairless. The safest way for you to enjoy shaving your legs is to present your case to your parents first!

How Parents Feel about Daughters Shaving Their Legs

"At first Mom said I was too young, then I talked her into letting me do it." Sheila, 7th grade

"Mom wanted me to shave because I have hairy legs." Patricia, 8th grade

"Mom wouldn't let me and it's embarrassing at gym in shorts having black hairs all over my legs." Heather, 7th grade

"Mom said that if I started I couldn't quit. She said I'd have to keep the razor clean so I didn't cut myself every time I shave." Caitlin, 8th grade

"I don't think it's that big of a deal but my mom does. She thinks I'm trying to grow up too fast." Vicki, 8th grade

"My parents said it was natural for a girl my age to start

shaving her legs." Dawn, 7th grade

"Mom surprised me and bought me an electric shaver. I was really surprised!" Judy, 7th grade

"I started shaving my legs in fourth grade without my parents knowing it. They didn't know 'til three months later. They didn't get mad. They didn't even say anything about it when they found out." Gabrielle, 7th grade

Underarm hair is a little more tricky to shave. It is helpful for most girls to have a demonstration from their moms, an older sister, or a friend who has been shaving for awhile. Like shaving your legs, if you don't do it right, you could wind up cutting yourself and learning too late that razor cuts in the armpits sting like crazy. (Especially when you apply deodorant!) I learned the hard way to make sure the blade was in straight and that if I shaved my underarms at night, any cuts would have a chance to heal before I put on deodorant the next morning.

Using Deodorant

Using deodorant is necessary now because your sweat glands have a stronger odor than when you were a child. As your sweat mixes with bacteria it smells very bad and is offensive. You can choose from many brands and types of deodorant: stick, roll-on, scented, unscented, and so on. Be sure to stock up on the kind you like best and use it every day.

The hair growth in the genital area may be the most embarrassing for you. But, like the other changes we have discussed, this is just a part of the natural process of growing older.

Making the Most of Shaping Up

Certain women, who probably remember their "body-changing" years, spend lots of time studying what clothing

25

styles look best on certain body designs. Check yourself out in front of a mirror. Decide what body design you have and which clothing style is right for you.

If you have a *thin body design,* you would look best in full skirts, blouses with full sleeves, bright colors, and large plaids and prints.

If you have an *overweight body design,* look for solid, dark, and neutral colors, or fabrics with small prints. Flared or A-line skirts are made for you, too.

Girls with a *tall body design* are fortunate, since most fashions are designed for you. You'll look great in bold fabrics, full sleeves, wide yokes, wide collars, wide belts. Your blouse and skirt colors should contrast each other. If you choose an outfit of the same color, break it up with a large belt, a bright scarf, flashy jewelry, or a jacket or sweater in contrasting color.

If you have a *short body design,* you would look great in outfits of the same color. Slightly flared skirts are perfect for you, as are short jackets, narrow belts, and dresses with high waists.

If you have *wide hips,* you can slim them down with skirts that have a slight gather, or skirts, dresses, and slacks with vertical lines. Other excellent choices include blouses with shoulder pads and loose vests.

If you have *narrow hips,* you would look good in full skirts, and skirts and slacks with hip pockets.

"Good Mood" Foods

Doctors say that the changes taking place in your body zap your energy and affect your moods. When you need a quick lift, snack on the following "Good Mood" foods. Show this list to your mom so she can have some of these foods available for you.

Popcorn

Milk

Cheese 'n crackers
Nuts
Bagels
Low-fat yogurt
Cereal
Juice
Raw sunflower seeds
Fresh fruits
Hard-cooked eggs
Dried fruits
Peanut butter on whole grain bread
Celery stuffed with peanut butter or cream cheese

A Different Kind of Feeling

You probably have all kinds of new feelings about your body changes. God created these feelings when he designed your body. They are important parts of you.

When you were small, it was normal for you to explore and to enjoy parts of your body by touching them. It was a good feeling. Before you reached junior high and you were still getting acquainted with your body, you may have discovered, through exploration, a special place around your vagina that gave you a different kind of feeling when you touched it.

The first time you touched your special place and experienced this new feeling, you may have felt guilty or scared. You were afraid to talk to anyone about it because you didn't know if anyone else had discovered the same thing about her body.

Here are some facts you may want to know about this special place and the feelings you have about it.

1. This special place of yours is called the "clitoris." It has many sensitive "touch" nerves in it. Touching your special place is called *masturbation*.

2. Masturbation doesn't hurt your body.

3. Most girls don't make masturbation a life-long practice. It's only one of the ways they use to explore their new body feelings.

4. Exploring your new body feelings by masturbation is a private thing.

5. You are normal if you do masturbate.

6. You are normal if you don't masturbate.

7. Most kids don't talk about masturbation to anyone.

8. Remember, "God saw *everything* he made and it was *all* good!" Part of "everything" is the special feelings you get while you're exploring your body parts.

> *What Some Girls Have Said about Masturbation*
> "I never heard anyone talk about it so I thought I was the only one who did it." Christie, 9th grade
> "Am I weird for doing it?" Alyssa, 8th grade
> "There's something about it that's very embarrassing." Kara, 10th grade
> "I don't want it to harm my insides." Laura, 7th grade

Handling Your Changes and Feelings

You're probably spending (or are going to spend) lots of time taking care of your complexion during your body-changing years. You may be experimenting with new hairstyles and makeup. You may be exercising more and trying not to eat food that manufactures pimples. All of this is great! It's important to take care of your body. But God added another part to your design to make you complete. These Words tell you what is most important: "Don't be concerned about the outward beauty that depends on jewelry, or beautiful clothes, or hair arrangement. *Be beautiful inside,* in your hearts, with the lasting charm of a gentle and quiet spirit which is so special to God" (1 Peter 3:3-4, emphasis added).

Question: How can I be beautiful inside?

Answer: You discover what you were designed to be and do, then you go for it!

Sounds easy, doesn't it? Well, it is . . . until you start saying "I wish *I* could be like _____," filling in the blank with the name of anyone you feel is better than you. This story may help you jump over the hurdle of comparing yourself to others.

> *A duck, a rabbit, and a squirrel got together and planned to take classes in running, climbing, swimming, and flying. Everyone had to take all the classes.*
>
> *The duck did great in the swimming class, but he made terrible grades in climbing and running. The rabbit made his best grades in running, but he injured his leg muscles in climbing class. The squirrel beat everyone in climbing class, but he failed flying class because the teacher insisted he start on the ground instead of in a tree.*
>
> *Here's what the three students learned: A duck is designed to swim,* not *to climb and run; a rabbit is designed to run,* not *to climb or swim; a squirrel is designed to climb,* not *to fly. They had wasted time and energy trying to be like someone else!*

Crazy story, but it tells you something special about that other more important part of your design: No one else has been designed to do or be what God has designed *you* to do or be. When you try to be like someone else you make yourself miserable. You expect something different of yourself than God designed you to be or do. When you do this, you wind up being a "fake."

> *"Everyone liked this girl. She was popular
> so I thought everyone would think the
> same about me if I hung around her. It
> didn't work."* Cheri, 8th grade.

Instead of thinking about what you can't do, think about the things you *can* do. Maybe you're too shy to run for a class office at school, but you love to spend hours making posters and campaigning for the kids you want to get elected. You may not get the lead in the drama productions, but you can help make the scenery, locate costumes, or make sure the makeup gets done right.

No one may ever nominate you to be homecoming queen, but you *know* you can get kids working together to build floats for the queens to ride on in the parades. You may not be interested in being editor of the school newspaper, but you'll spend hours selling ads so there will be money to print the paper.

Maybe you aren't a cheerleader, but everyone who sits by you at ball games knows you're the team spirit. You can scream louder than anyone else when your team is winning or losing.

You really *are* on the same level as the girls whose names make the headlines in the school paper and are announced over the loudspeaker. School leaders wouldn't be leaders if they didn't have you to help them get elected.

You have the special design of a person who others count on. You're necessary. You're missed if you aren't around. You're important to your school because you're doing what God designed you to do — and that makes you beautiful inside.

Think about the following Words: "God has given each of us the ability to do certain things well" (Romans 12:6), and "God has given . . . you some special abilities; be sure to use them to help each other" (1 Peter 4:10).

The following Words were written to a group of people in a church in biblical times, but they can be used to describe you and the other kids in your school:

The body [school] has many parts, not just one part. If the foot says, "I am not a part of the body [school] because I am not a hand [a leader, a football star]," that does not make it any less a part of the body [the school]. . . . God has made . . . many parts for our bodies and has put each part [person] just where he wants it.

What a strange thing a body [school] would be if it had only one part [one follower and the rest leaders]! . . . And some of the parts [people] that seem weakest and least important are really the most necessary. . . . So God has put the body [school] together in such a way that extra honor and care are given to those that might otherwise seem less important. . . . Now here is what I'm trying to say: All of you together [at school] are . . . a separate and necessary part. (1 Corinthians 12:14-15, 18-19, 22, 24, 27)

A Few Ways to Be Beautiful Inside

1. Slip in a compliment to your parents once in a while.
2. Declare "Be Nice to Brother (or Sister, or Teacher, or Parent, or Self) Day" once every three months.
3. Say hi to someone you think you don't like.
4. Invite a new girl in your class to your home. Ask some of your friends to come, too, so they can get to know the new girl.
5. Write an older person a note and tell that person something you like about him or her. (How about a grandparent, an older friend of your family's, or an older person at church?)
6. Take a walk by yourself and think about the good

things you see in people or the good things you've seen people do.

7. Talk to the shy kids in your class.
8. Once a week don't let your mind have a bad thought for an hour about anyone or anything.
9. When you have a negative thought about yourself, replace it immediately with at least two positive things about yourself.
10. Practice thinking about what you *can* do, not what you can't do.

Whatever you are experiencing, remember that right now is the most dramatic time of change in your life (other than the day you came from that safe, warm place in your mom's womb and let out a squall to let everyone know you had arrived with God's stamp of approval). Read everything you can about the physical and emotional changes you'll be experiencing. Look up information about how your body works. Watch, feel, and enjoy yourself as the changes take place.

Some girls want to get all their changes over with so they can see their finished product—but the steps it takes to go from girl to woman take more time than fixing instant oatmeal or microwaving a potato. So for now, believe you're doing a great job of shaping up!

Any time you think or say, "I wish I could be like . . .," read these Words: "God . . . is able to do far more [with my life] than [I] would ever dare to ask or even dream of — infinitely beyond [my] highest prayers, desires, thoughts, or hopes" (Ephesians 3:20).

It's true. God has designed you to do some special things that only you can do.

So get ready.

Get set.

Go for it!

TWO

Secret
Feelings
about
Having
Periods

> *Dear Diary,*
> *Today I started my period for the first time. I let out a*
> *scream when I saw I'd started. I thought,* Wow! *Then I*
> *started getting cramps and I didn't think having a period*
> *was so great.*
>
> *Lindey*

Most girls wonder what having a period will feel like. They wonder when they'll start having it and where they'll be when it starts. My daughter Dana remembered every detail about her first period.

> *My first period started the summer after the seventh*
> *grade. It started on a Saturday. What a relief! I was*
> *always afraid it would start while I was at school or out*
> *somewhere else. I woke up and had a little bit of blood in*
> *my pants. I called for my mom to come and I told her. I*
> *remember she was very gentle and patient with me and*
> *acted very calm . . . that helped me to feel the same way.*
> *I had known about periods for quite a while, and I*
> *knew I would have one. When I saw the evidence I*
> *thought it* might *be my period, but I was scared that*

maybe it was something else. When I called my mom, she confirmed I had started my period.

I was really excited! Other girls I knew had already started and it was almost a status symbol, a sign that you had grown up. I thought I would be "a woman" when I started.

My mom took me to the bathroom and showed me how to keep myself clean and showed me how to put on a sanitary napkin. It was huge. Mom showed me how to wrap my used napkins and told me how often I should change. After I got all fixed up, I went back to bed to lay down. I remember feeling so happy.

Mom told me that this was the way our bodies got prepared for having babies. I liked that. I just lay there thinking that I had gotten my period! I wanted to tell my girlfriends, but instead I just kept it a secret.

Even after your mom delivers her "Everything You Need to Know about Having a Period" lecture series, after she puts books about menstruation in strange places around the house for you to stumble over, even after the school nurse tells you what your mom forgot to tell you, you may *still* have some unanswered questions about what it will feel like to have a period.

How Some Girls Felt before They Started Their Periods

"I wanted to know more about it. At first I didn't like the idea that blood would literally drip from me in that area. But then, I really wanted to have my period." Marj, 7th grade

"When I first heard about having a period I thought, 'It isn't true. Someone's joking with me.' It scared me to death. I thought it would hurt really bad." Amy, 9th grade

"I couldn't believe you bled for at least five days. First, I was scared, then when all my friends started, I could hardly wait. Every day I looked but nothing was there." Elaine, 8th grade

"I didn't want it and I was gonna put it off as long as I possibly could." Cindy, 10th grade

"I really didn't give it much thought. I figured I'd deal with it when it came. I looked forward to it." Edie, 10th grade

"I hated the whole subject. I thought having a period would be embarrassing and everyone would know I was on my period. It's not fair!" Debra, 8th grade

"It sounded nasty and I wondered if it would hurt." Ashley, 7th grade

"I thought it sounded grown up and I wished I'd start. My sister and her friends had started. They told me it was awful and I was lucky I didn't have mine, but I still wanted my period to start!" Darlene, 9th grade

"Those little booklets they hand out at school are gross." Tracy, 7th grade

"I thought it would be great! It meant I would be a woman. I had heard of cramps and hoped I wouldn't have them. I heard periods lasted five days." Jeannie, 8th grade

Starting Your Period

It would be great if every girl could know for sure that she would start her first period at home, on a weekend, with no cramping, a light flow, and all of her "period stuff" ready to use. Too bad our bodies usually don't cooperate that way. The two biggest fears girls wrote about on their question-naires regarding starting their periods were (1) not know-ing where they would be when their periods started and (2) not being prepared.

One eighth grade girl wrote, "My first period happened at school. I wrapped my jacket around my waist. I went to the nurse's office. I was so embarrassed. I cried because the blood had leaked onto my slacks." A seventh grade girl wrote, "I was on a vacation with one of my friends and her family when my period started. I was totally unprepared and too embarrassed to ask someone to help me. I just kept folding thick wads of toilet paper in my underwear. I was miserable. Girls should be told that they can ask another woman for help."

Here are some tips to help you be more prepared for the time your period will start. If your period starts at school and you're too embarrassed to ask a teacher to be excused from class, write a note saying, "I think I've started my period. May I be excused?"

If you aren't prepared with pads and none are available at school, get permission to call one of your parents or an available family friend and ask them to bring your "period stuff" to you. (Ask your mom to help you choose an available friend ahead of time, and ask her to have the necessary supplies on hand so she'll be prepared to help you.)

How Some Girls Felt about Their First Period

"It really wasn't that bad!" Erin, 9th grade

"I thought something bad was wrong with me and no one had ever had this problem before. All I could think of was wanting to get rid of it." Darla, 7th grade

"I cried and cried when I first started because I just knew I was diseased!" Amy, 8th grade

"It didn't bother me real bad because my mom and I used to talk about it all the time. I got a book on pregnancy [that] went through the steps of menstruation." Carole, 8th grade

"My period started when I was in seventh grade. I was at home. At first, I thought I was having diarrhea, so I changed my underwear. I called my mom to my bedroom and she said I had started. I thought the blood should've been red but it wasn't. That's why I wasn't sure what was going on. Mom gave me a pad. It felt like a brick when I started walking. I kept thinking, 'There's got to be something better than this.' I started getting cramps and I thought that no one but me had ever had cramps that felt like this. I felt terrible!" Kari, 8th grade

"I went to my friend's house after school and I told her I thought I had started my period. She kept asking, 'How do you know?' We were too embarrassed to ask her mom for some pads so we sneaked some out of her bathroom. The next day I was still bleeding so I knew I had started." Yvonne, 10th grade

"I thought I was dying and then I realized I was on my period." Kellie, 7th grade

"I really wanted my period, but after I got it I wanted to give it away." Julie, 8th grade

"Having my period start made me feel like a whole different person." Annette, 8th grade

"My mom wasn't home so I told my older sister and we both cracked up laughing." Laurie, 7th grade

What makes one girl "crack up laughing" when she starts her first period and another girl say, "I hate it. I got so mad. I cried and stayed in my room all weekend"? A girl might laugh when she starts her periods because the long wait is over and she has finally gotten her answer to what a period feels like. It's also a definite sign to a girl that she isn't a little kid anymore.

The "I hate it" group thinks periods are a nuisance because they usually show up at the most inconvenient times, such as on vacations or dates, or at sleepovers and swim parties. One eighth grader wrote, "My period always comes at the wrong time. I wish I'd never started."

These "hate it" girls don't like the hassle of having to carry around things like tampons and pads as they wait for their period to show up. Also, they're afraid some male clown will grab their purses and empty out the "evidence" for all the other guys to see.

Different reactions might also have something to do with the way a girl's first period goes: whether she has lots of cramping, whether her flow is light or heavy, whether she has her "period stuff" ready when her period starts. The way in which other girls or family members talk about having a period can affect the way a girl feels about menstruation.

How Moms Feel about Their Daughters' First Periods

I'll never forget my mom's reaction to my first period. I had gone to the bathroom and noticed a small brown spot in my underwear. It didn't look like blood, but I did wonder if it had anything to do with a period. I went into the kitchen where Mom was preparing dinner and I said, "I think I've started." She didn't even ask, "Started what?" She made some comments about periods and gave me my "equipment." She didn't make a big deal out of it. I was so glad she reacted that way. If her mouth had dropped open, or if she had gotten a wild look on her face or started crying, I probably would've thought I was in the beginning stages of some incurable disease.

Most moms will do all they can to make their daughters' first period pain- and embarrassment-free. A mother's first reaction can make a big difference in the way a girl feels about having her period.

How Some Girls' Mothers Reacted

"It was after school and I went to the bathroom. I noticed that my urine was bloody and I yelled for Mom to come. She came in and said, 'Puberty has struck.' She got some pads for me and said that it's going to happen every month and nothing is wrong." Elyse, 9th grade

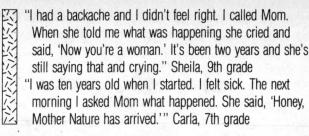

"I had a backache and I didn't feel right. I called Mom. When she told me what was happening she cried and said, 'Now you're a woman.' It's been two years and she's still saying that and crying." Sheila, 9th grade

"I was ten years old when I started. I felt sick. The next morning I asked Mom what happened. She said, 'Honey, Mother Nature has arrived.'" Carla, 7th grade

One mother told me that her daughter didn't start her periods until she was sixteen. All of her friends had started and it embarrassed her daughter when they kept asking her if she had started. She had grown taller but her body still had the same shape it had when she was in elementary school. She was a beautiful girl, but she was self-conscious because she thought her flat body announced to everyone that she hadn't started her periods. It's too bad no one told her that she was beautiful and *normal,* even though she hadn't started her period yet.

Your mom may or may not make a big deal out of you starting your period, but it probably *is* a big deal to both of you because menstruation is giving your body the "go ahead" to start shaping up and preparing for another beautiful part of God's design for you.

It doesn't matter when you start, or how your period treats you — whether you have cramps or not, whether you start early or not, whether you have a heavy or light flow — whatever your body does is normal for you. There is no "right" or "wrong" way to have a period. Some girls start when they are ten or eleven years old. Others don't start until they are older.

What's Normal?

Normal is having a period every month . . . or skipping some months.

"I missed a month and I thought I was pregnant, but I knew I hadn't done anything." Dawn, 9th grade

"My periods were irregular at first. Sometimes I'd miss a month and then an extra period would start before my twenty-eight days were up." Terri, 10th grade

Normal is a heavy flow . . . or a light flow.

"I was in the bathroom and I felt like I was growing up, but I felt gross because my flow was very heavy. My Dad was the only one home and I was very embarrassed." Traci, 8th grade

"My flow was medium and pretty easy to handle. I've worn tampons since my first period." Delores, 8th grade

"I was shocked and I thought, *Crud, I have to have this for the rest of my life.* But my first period was real light and I didn't feel it until I got home. I was glad about that." Jeanette, 7th grade

Normal is having cramps . . . or not having cramps.

"Some months I'd have cramps in my lower back and stomach." Linda, 8th grade

"I had cramps and I took aspirin and the cramps wouldn't go away. I thought that maybe I wouldn't have them anymore, but boy, was I shocked the next month. I was saying, 'God make this go away and never come back.'" Leslie, 9th grade

"Sometimes I have cramps and sometimes I don't." Nadine, 7th grade

Normal is starting your period earlier . . . or later than your friends.

"I didn't want to tell my friends that I had started because I was afraid they'd treat me like I was from outer space." Nancy, 7th grade

"I started in the sixth grade. When one of my friends started in the seventh grade I told her it was neat that we had that in common!" Rachel, 9th grade

"I was kind of glad to have it because I was one of the last ones in my class to start." Leone, 9th grade

"I had been waiting a long time for my period, so I was excited when I got it." Jodie, 9th grade

Why You Have Periods

You've probably spent lots of time thinking about having your period. It might help you get used to the idea of having monthly periods if you understand *why* you have them. There is a definite reason why girls have periods: as soon as you've had your first period, your body gives the signal that you are able to become pregnant. Wow!

It's as normal as breathing to want to know all you can about how women get pregnant. You've probably already talked with your friends about it—and all of you may have different ideas about it. You may have even looked up the words *sex* and *human reproduction* in the dictionary or in an encyclopedia.

The more you read the more you probably realized pregnancy is a miracle. It probably seems kind of strange to think now that when you and your future husband decide you are ready to accept the responsibility of a baby, your body will have the privilege of making and growing a brand new little person.

Maybe your parents have explained the miracle of birth to you. If so, that's great! Especially since having a period is the first step toward eventually being able to become a mother. But some parents really aren't comfortable telling their daughters about sexual intercourse and reproduction.

An eighth grade girl said that one evening her dad told her to come into the living room. She thought she had done something wrong. Her dad smiled and said, "We need to have a little talk." He said that he felt it was time for her to know how women got pregnant.

All she remembers was that he said something about a

41

"seed," an "egg," and "intercourse." She was so embarrassed that she stopped him by telling him that she already knew about all that stuff. But she really *didn't* know, so she started getting her information from books and from her friends.

Most parents want their daughters to know about pregnancy and how having periods fits into that part of a woman's design. If no one has told you *why* you have periods, I would like to have the privilege of telling you. A verse from the Bible says that "[God] made all the delicate, inner parts of [your] body" (Psalm 139:13). Two of the many reasons God designed your body the way he did were so that it would have periods and so that it would produce babies. It's very important for you to know all you can about the female "inner parts" of your body and what they are designed to do.

A Girl's Inventory

Close to your brain is your pituitary gland. When this gland starts functioning it releases chemical substances called *hormones*. The female hormones are called *progesterone* and *estrogen*. When these hormones are released into your bloodstream, it lets your body know it is ready to start having periods.

To cause a period to happen, God designed women in a very special way. That design includes:

Two ovaries — internal organs about the size of a large almond shell.

One uterus or "womb" — when a woman isn't pregnant, this organ looks kind of like a flat, three-inch long pear.

Two fallopian (fa-lope-ee-un) tubes — these connect the ovaries and the uterus.

One vagina — the opening from the uterus to the outside of your body. This opening is between your legs and is where the blood from your period leaves your body.

Also included in your inventory are the egg cells which are stored in your ovaries. You were born with approximately 150,000 to 500,000 egg cells in each ovary. These cells are so small that if you placed 4,000 of them side by side they would measure less than one inch.

It takes about a month for one of these eggs to ripen. After approximately fourteen days, one of your ovaries (the two ovaries take turns each month) releases an egg and it heads down the tube and into your uterus (womb).

If the egg doesn't unite with a sperm during sexual intercourse (intercourse is explained in detail in chapter three), the blood starts to collect on the inside of your uterus. When the blood is ready to leave your body, it begins to break away from the inside wall of the uterus. Then it travels down the vagina and out through the opening between your legs. Result: Your period.

The blood usually drips slowly from your vagina and during the three to seven days of your period, approximately 4 ounces (1/2 cup) of blood leaves your body. The amount of blood can be different each month and still be normal. After this cycle is over, another egg cell starts to ripen and within approximately twenty-eight days you will have your next period.

The basic facts about periods are: God designed your body to have periods so that your body could prepare itself to have a baby. In God's perfect design this was to happen only after you met, dated, fell in love with, and married the right man.

You probably have already read (or will be reading in books or seeing on TV) that our society doesn't take God's plan about having sex or babies seriously. There are many people who seem to believe it's OK to have sex if you're not married. Some even feel it's OK to have babies if you're not married. That's why it's important for you to know about and believe in God's complete design for you. You need to remember about your body and discover God's plan for you.

When you reach the age when you are ready to start your period, you are really in the first stage of that special design. Remember, though, this is only one stage that is preparing your body to carry out one of God's many wonderful plans for women: having a baby.

Twelve Great Tips

1. On a calendar, circle the day you start your period. Count ahead twenty-eight days from that date and circle that day. This will help you know the approximate starting day of your next period. If you do this for several months, it can also help you see if you're on a schedule different from a twenty-eight day cycle.

2. Though it doesn't happen all that often, many of us worry about blood leaking through our clothes during our periods. To give yourself some peace of mind, forget you have white slacks, skirts, or shorts when you are close to starting (or during) your period. Dark clothing helps conceal blood if it should leak through your clothing. Also, let a close friend know you're on your period. Ask her to check the back of your clothes through the day in case the blood has leaked through.

3. When menstrual blood comes in contact with air, it makes an odor. So be sure to change your pad often (you'll know how often after you've had a few periods) and wash your genital area once or twice each day.

4. Have a plan. For example, fill in the blanks: "If I start my period at school, I will _____" or "If I start my period at a party, I will _____."

5. Experiment with different pad sizes to decide which size is most comfortable for you. If you decide to wear tampons, certain doctors caution against wearing one any longer than four to six hours at a time (because of

Toxic Shock Syndrome). Also, do not wear tampons through the night; use a pad instead. If you have any discomfort wearing a tampon, switch to wearing pads.

6. It might make you feel more secure to purchase a container designed to hold pads or tampons for your purse.

7. Check out the school rest rooms and other public rest rooms for the location of sanitary pad and tampon machines. Carry "emergency" change in your purse to use in the machines in case you start your period unexpectedly.

8. If your period makes you crabby or if you have cramps, let your parents know how you're feeling. You may be surprised at how understanding they can be! If you have cramps, ask your doctor to recommend a mild pain-relieving medicine. Many of these may be purchased over the counter without a prescription. Use a heating pad on your stomach and/or back, and get as much rest as possible.

9. Another thing to try if you're crabby is taking 100 mg. of Vitamin B6 once a day. Start taking these vitamins fourteen days from the start of your last period and continue taking them until your next period starts. Also, avoid sugar in foods such as cookies, soda, and candy, which can cause irritability.

10. Stay away from lots of salt starting ten days before you start your period. Salt causes your body to store water, which can cause your breasts, abdomen, and the blood vessels in your head to swell.

11. Read everything you can about periods. The more information you have, the more comfortable and accepting you will be with your periods.

12. Remember, no matter how bad your periods might treat you, having a period is *not* fatal!

THREE

Secret
Feelings
about
Boys

Dear Diary,
P.H. is so cute! And smart, too. He's in two of my classes,
and he always has the right answers. I thought he was
going to talk to me yesterday. I wanted to crawl away
and hide because I just knew I'd say something stupid.
But he didn't talk to me. I'm not even sure he knows I
exist.

Lindey

In fourth grade, the part of my day that I liked best was the school lunch hour. After eating lunch, the boys and girls met on the playground and started playing "chase." The girls started running, and the boys started chasing them.

In fifth grade, I couldn't explain how I felt about boys. I only knew I felt different about them than I ever had before. The boys must have been going through some of the same changes in their feelings about girls because they began hanging around each other more and our chase games ended.

The first official couple of our sixth grade class was Tommy and Mary Lou. They were more physically developed than the rest of us. The teacher always sat them across the room from each other, but even being six rows apart didn't stop them from staring at each other during class. Tommy winked at Mary Lou all the time. Then her face would turn red and she'd smile.

In seventh grade, a new boy, D.S., moved to town. He was *so* good looking. I wrote a lot about D.S. in my diary. I hated myself for feeling shy and awkward around him. When I did get a chance to say something to him, I was always afraid I said the wrong thing and made him think I *didn't* like him.

During that year, some of us began having Friday night parties in our homes. Games were the best part of the evenings. One game we played was "Post Office." The girls stayed in one room, the boys went to another room. Each group passed out papers with numbers on them. The girls got to walk around the block with the boy who had the same number as theirs. I discovered later that the boys had ways of finding out which girls had which numbers, and the boys switched their numbers until they got the girl they wanted to walk with.

I always hoped I would get D.S. as my partner. The funny thing was, as badly as I wanted to be D.S.'s partner, I *didn't* want it. The thought of being that close to him or having to talk to him actually made me so nervous it upset my stomach!

When D.S. moved to another town during the tenth grade, I knew I'd never get a chance to let him know how much I liked him. I had such confused feelings that I couldn't even write in my diary how I felt about his leaving.

Confused Feelings

Having these kinds of feelings about boys is normal. My daughter Beth told me how she experienced many confused feelings about a certain boy when she was in junior high. She said she could remember jumping back and forth from like to love to hate feelings for B.H.

Her first diary entry about him read, "Dear Diary, I like B.H. He gave me a gerbil." Later she told her older sister that she liked B.H. as a boyfriend.

After Beth was sure she liked B.H. as a boyfriend, one of her girl friends (C.T.) showed up and tried to get B.H. to notice her. "C.T. smiles at B.H. all the time," Beth wrote in her diary. "I don't know what to do. I really liked B.H." Then, a month later, she wrote, "I don't like B.H. anymore. He's a real weirdo because he thinks he's something great. I love M.A. now because he's so funny. He's really something special."

One of Beth's last diary entries expressed her confused feelings: "I'm so mad at C.T. I don't know what to do. I really and truly like B.H. It sounds crazy, but it's how I feel. I'm afraid when all of us kids go to music camp this summer, B.H. will hang around with C.T. I'm so confused that I can't go to sleep. B.H. and I have such good times together at church, at my house and at camps . . . just about everywhere."

You may be having trouble explaining some of your confused feelings about boys, too. You know they're not the same feelings you had in nursery school and kindergarten—but you aren't sure why they changed! It's like someone gave you an eye transplant one night while you were asleep. When you woke up the next day, boys started looking *very* interesting.

You want someone to help you understand why you're feeling differently about boys. Not even your best friend can come up with an explanation that makes sense. All you know is that certain boys look better and more interesting than other boys.

The way boys are acting now, you wonder if they get together before school and plan to ignore all girls that day.

Then the next day they seem to have decided it's "Make-Dumb-Remarks-to-Girls Day." The more interesting boys act like you haven't been born yet; the uninteresting ones seem to have developed the bad habit of following you like a twenty-four-hour shadow, doing dumb things to get you to notice them.

Why Boys Act the Way They Do

It's normal for boys in junior high to act strangely. You see, they are going through changes and experiencing confusing emotions, too. You need to know *how* they are changing and why their changes make some of them act the way they do around girls.

A boy has the same "button" close to his brain (the pituitary gland) that you have. When this button is punched it does the same thing your pituitary gland does: it releases hormones into the bloodstream. The principal male hormone is called *testosterone*. (Remember, your female hormones are progesterone and estrogen.) The new production of testosterone affects *100 percent* of a boy's body parts. When testosterone is turned on it not only changes a boy physically, it also wakes up his male sex drive. This wake-up call makes girls . . . *all girls* . . . look very interesting. And *that's* why boys start acting strange around girls.

You're definitely going to be an important part of the boys' new feelings. That's why you need to know how God designed boys and how your feelings about them are different from their feelings about you.

It may embarrass you to read about (much less to say aloud) the names of certain male body parts. That's OK. Certain body parts of a guy *are* private. The problem is that some people make so many jokes about these body parts that they sound nasty or indecent. These kind of jokes make you feel like you're trespassing in forbidden areas when you read about or say the names of the male sex organs. Remember, though, these body parts are just as much a part of a boy's design as your female parts are a part of your design. It's important to learn about the way God designed boys' bodies. This will help you understand how the changes boys experience can affect their feelings about and attitudes toward girls.

A Boy's Inventory

A boy comes into the world with an inventory of:

One penis — This is a tube-like part on the outside of his body through which he urinates. Later, it also becomes the place where sperm cells leave his body. (Sperm cells are the tiny cells manufactured in a boy's testicles.)

Two testicles — These are a boy's sex organs (your sex organs are the ovaries). The testicles have two jobs: they make male sex hormones (testosterone) and they make and store sperm cells (just like your ovaries store egg cells).

One scrotum (skro-tum) — This is a bag of skin under and behind a boy's penis. It holds his testicles.

One prostate (prah-state) *gland and seminal vesicles* (seh-mi-nul ve-sick-uls) — These are located inside a boy's abdomen. They join forces to make a milky, white fluid in which the sperm cells float.

When the hormone testosterone is released into a boy's bloodstream, his body begins performing some quick changing acts. One of the most obvious changes which might give him trouble and embarrassment is his voice change. When a boy this age talks he never knows if his voice will squeak, crackle, or jump up or down two octaves. This could be why some guys put off talking to certain girls — they don't know what their voices will decide to do while they're talking.

Other body changing acts cause boys to get taller and more muscular. They start to grow soft whiskers. They want to shave, but they're not quite sure when to start. Hair begins to grow on their armpits, chest, arms, legs, and the area around the penis. Some guys consider this new hair to be a locker room "status symbol."

Just like girls, some boys experience their changes at an early age. Others impatiently wait for the first signs of new hair to arrive. They still have hairless bodies and they hate to change clothes for P.E. in front of the "status symbol" guys.

One of boys' newest changes can be very upsetting and even scary for them. That is when they start having what are called *wet dreams.* A wet dream happens when the seminal fluid that contains sperm cells leaves a boy's body through his penis, usually while he is asleep. It's important to understand that having wet dreams is a normal part of the physical growth taking place in a boy's body.

The first time a wet dream happens to an uninformed boy, he might think he has wet his bed. That's pretty scary and embarrassing . . . probably as scary as when you wake up and discover you have started your first period during the night.

You know you don't make your period start. A boy doesn't make his body have wet dreams, either. It does it on its own because of the new production of his pituitary gland. Wet dreams are a normal part of a boy's change. These "dreams" stir up all kinds of feelings and fantasies about girls, but having these feelings and fantasies doesn't necessarily mean he wants to act them out.

These feelings are so new to boys that it could be the answer to why they act differently around girls. They are trying to figure out how to deal with what's happening inside of them. They wonder what does and doesn't work to get a girl's attention. So if a boy you know has been acting weird around you, he may be saying, "Hey! I'm a boy. Notice me. I just might be the type of guy you could like."

What Guys Fantasize about Girls

"Having lots of girls liking me and all they want to do is be around me and kiss me."

"Being liked by a girl I know I don't have a chance with."

"Girls hanging all over me."

"Being married to the prettiest girl in school."

"Having sex."

"Being stranded with a girl on an island."

"Dancing together."

"Walking along the beach."

"Seeing girls in bikinis at the swimming pool."

"Having a romantic night with a girl."

Boy Types

Boys generally fall into two types: Type A, the type you really like and you want to like you; and Type B, the type you *don't* like and you hope don't like you. One of your biggest questions might be: How do I get Type A to like me? Girls have come up with all kinds of plans and strategies. Here are a few of the plans they use:

The "Here-I-Am-You-Lucky-Guy" plan.
"I walk in front of him and I follow him a lot."
"I flirt big time."
"I start a conversation with him."
"I act crazy so he'll notice me."
"I write notes to him."
"I call him on the telephone."
"I bump into him, and then I say, 'I didn't mean to.'"

The "Playing-it-Safe" plan.
"I try to talk to someone he hangs around with so that we'll run into each other."

"I get my friends to talk to him to find out if he likes me."

"I laugh at his jokes."

"I talk to the guy and smile a lot and see if he talks or smiles back! I call him sometime so maybe he'll think I like him and he'll be interested."

"I find out which halls he takes between classes and I just happen to bump into him."

The "Shy" plan.
"When I pass him in the halls at school I smile at him."

"I try to dress well so he'll notice me."

"I wish I could tell him how I feel about him but I can't!"

"I'm extremely self-conscious around him and basically ignore him when he's around."

"I try to act normal. It's too painful to act like someone I'm not."

The "I'm-Not-Ready-to-Start-Flirting" plan.
"I'm scared I'll say something stupid."

"I feel funny when I see this guy I like."

"My stomach jumps up and down."

"I get hyper and chills when I'm around him."

"I feel weird around boys."

On the questionnaire, many of the girls described Type A boys as boys who were friendly; easy to talk to and to be around; involved in sports, music, drama or other school activities; serious about their grades; and honest. These girls also wrote that Type A boys aren't show-offs, and that they treat girls like they're special. It also helps if Mr. Type A is "borderline" cute or handsome.

> *"I think I like him because of his gorgeous looks. I was blinded by blonde hair, muscles, and baby blue eyes. He didn't really notice me because I was so shy. I would put my foot in my mouth when I tried to talk to him." Dana, 8th grade*

Type B boys are boys whose bodies and voices are still waiting to change, or who aren't interested in girls (. . . yet), or who get their kicks by teasing and making dumb remarks to girls.

I remember standing close to some Type B guys one day in my eighth grade class. These boys were in a huddle and all of them were laughing. They broke their huddle slightly and I saw why they were laughing. They were passing around a picture of a nude girl that one of the guys had drawn. They must have wanted me to see why they were laughing so they could see my reaction. They got it! I could feel my face get hot and I wanted to crawl under the floor. The best thing I could have done was ignore them, but I didn't think of that at the time.

Girl Types

Boys are as busy making out girl-type lists as girls are making out their boy-type lists.

Guys describe Type A girls as girls who care about people, are fun to be with, are easy to talk to, dress and act like girls, have nice bodies and good looks, don't smoke or drink, and aren't overweight.

Boys say Type B girls are bossy or stuck-up, act tough, smoke and drink, show off their bodies, wear lots of make-up, and are loudmouths.

It's obvious that boys and girls are interested in the way each other's bodies are shaping up. You may think the only reason some boys don't notice you is because your body hasn't changed much. Read the boys' Type A list again. Many other things about you are attractive. Your smile, your attitudes, the way you talk and dress, your personality . . . It takes more than just a well-developed body to be a Type A.

Do some serious thinking about your personality. Think about the ways you treat people. How friendly are you?

How do you talk to or about people? The way you treat people may get (and keep) your name on a boy's Type A list.

Way to Go

Since fifth or sixth grade you've probably had your eye on certain guys. You liked one because he was good-looking. Then you'd like someone who was fun to be with, and his being good-looking wasn't so important anymore. You felt more relaxed around certain boys. Sometimes boys returned your like; sometimes they didn't. Other times you'd keep your "like" such a secret that the boy didn't even know you liked him.

> *"I keep as far away as I can from the guys I like. If they found out I liked them they'd probably throw up."* Cindy, 8th grade

With each new relationship with a guy, you decide what you do and don't like about him. That's great. You're doing it right.

Lots of girls wonder how they can really get to know a boy well. How can they find out if he's the kind of boy they'd like to know better and maybe even want to have as a first date? The best way to go with your new feelings and interests about *any* boy is S-L-O-W! By taking things slowly you will have time to watch the boy and see if he fits into your Type A list. You should be choosy, even if it means fewer dates. You're special, so you can afford to be choosy (and you can't afford not to be!).

Make a checklist of at least five things you like about a guy. Decide what number (between one and ten, ten being the best) you'll give him for personality, good morals, being a Christian, manners, personal appearance, the way he treats girls, and anything else that's important to you. Do your addition and then don't go out with a guy that doesn't score high in all of your categories!

How You Get To Know a Guy

OK. You've made your checklist and you've found a boy you want to get to know better. House parties are a great way to get to know a certain guy. He can be one of several people you invite to a party without him knowing how you feel about him. If he accepts your invitation and comes to the party, watch how he interacts with your friends to see if he's as great as you think he is. These parties can help you know when to scratch some of the guys off your Type A list. They may even help you see when you should transfer some of your Type Bs to your Type A list.

At the end of this chapter you will find some games you can play at weekend parties that will give you healthy, physical contact with boys. These games can also help you understand more about the new feelings you're having for boys. Try some of them at your next girl/boy house party.

Group Dates

Suppose a guy has passed your Type A test and has responded to your interest by coming to a house party. A good next step is group dating. This kind of dating will be more fun for both of you until you get to know each other better and you find out what you have in common. I remember a time I went out alone with a boy and ended up wishing we'd gone on a group date instead. I didn't know the boy very well, and we hadn't planned anything special to do on the date. So when we ran out of things to talk about we started kissing. I didn't even enjoy kissing him because he was floating somewhere between my Type A and Type B lists.

Get your mind busy working for you. You'll be surprised how many things you can plan for group dates. Here are some suggestions for things you can do with a group: jogging, hiking, swimming, bowling, skating, tennis, roller skating, biking, racquetball, canoeing, volleyball, horseback riding, going to the zoo, going to a movie, renting a movie and having a "home theater" night (popcorn and all), going to a concert, going on a picnic (be sure the guys bring some of the food), and having a tree-climbing contest. You won't be an expert at all of these activities, but that's OK. Besides, it does something for a guy's ego to help you learn how to do something new.

Drag out the old table games when you can't go outside. They're great fun with a group. Create competition between girls and boys or between couples. Charades is always a good group game. If you live in an area where there's lots of snow during the winter months, try sleigh riding, skiing, ice skating, making snow sculptures, or building snow forts and having a wild snowball fight.

Be creative. There's no better way to get to know someone than by doing something fun . . . and maybe a little different.

Now What?

So far so good. You asked a special guy to one of your house parties and he passes the first crucial test. You are still interested in him and he becomes interested in you. So you've been group dating for a while, and he's still passing the test. Now comes the big question: How do you know you're ready for a solo date? You *do* know you don't want to rush into it and end up disappointed.

My first solo date wasn't fun. I thought I could hardly wait for D.T. to ask me out. He was tall, borderline handsome, and drove a great car. I had other girls ask him if he liked me. When he found out I liked him, he asked me out. I asked a friend what I could talk to him about on the date. She told me to talk to him about his car.

When D.T. picked me up, I asked him some fairly intelligent questions about his car — but that only took up five minutes of our date. I spent the rest of the evening trying to think of ways to keep him from walking me to the door and kissing me.

He *did* walk me to the door. We stood there about ten seconds before I mumbled, "I had a nice time." Then I pulled the door open and went inside. As I shut the door I knew I was ready to go back to group dating.

Before you go out the door on that special solo date, there are some very important facts you should know *and* believe about relationships between boys and girls.

Boy Facts

This is an important section. I hope you will read it often while you're in junior high, especially before you start dating. The facts in this section show you the big differences between girls' and boys' new feelings about each other and explain how these feelings affect and fit into your relationships.

Boys Feel Differently about Sex Than Girls Do

A boy's new sexual feelings wake up quickly. Simple things like making eye contact with a girl, talking to other guys about girls, watching the way a girl walks or dresses can wake up these feelings. You can imagine what it does to a boy's feelings when he sees a girl wearing tight clothing or a bikini that exposes 99 percent of her anatomy.

Some boys wrote on their questionnaires that seeing girls in revealing or tight clothes makes them feel "embarrassed," "weird," or "uneasy." Others wrote that they felt "disgust" and they "lost respect for the girl" who shows off her body this way. The guys whose hormones are super active said that they can't keep their eyes off girls who dress that way. They felt "desperate," "horny," and "excited."

It's normal to want certain guys to notice you. But you want them to notice you for the right reasons. What you wear can either help a boy keep his new sexual feelings in the normal zone or help them go crazy!

Think about the following Words. You may even want to memorize them and say them to yourself each time you stand in front of your closet and decide what you'll wear. After you put on your outfit, stand in front of your mirror and see if it passes the test.

> *[I must] carefully protect from the eyes of others those parts that should not be seen, while of course the parts that may be seen do not require this special care.*
> *(1 Corinthians 12:23-24)*
>
> *[My] unpresentable parts are treated with greater modesty which [my] more presentable parts do not require. (1 Corinthians 12:23-24, RSV)*

A Boy's Sexual Feelings Might Wake Up Even When a Girl's Clothes Don't Expose 99 Percent of Her Anatomy

There was a boy in the eighth grade who liked a girl in his class. He sat with her in the church worship services each Sunday. One Sunday as he was sitting by her, he fainted. He fainted again the next Sunday. He was rushed to the hospital and had all types of tests run, including a brain scan. The doctors couldn't find anything physically wrong with him. Then his doctor talked with him and found out that just sitting by this girl and having a slight physical contact with her excited him so much that he fainted.

Every boy who likes you won't faint when he sits by you, but this true story might help you understand how much normal sexual feelings can affect some boys!

Kissing Any Girl Wakes Up a Guy's Sexual Feelings

When a girl touches a boy's thigh, puts her arm around his waist, or gives him a light kiss, his sexual feelings can get a wake-up call.

I was in marching band during junior high. One night the band members were on a school bus returning home from a football game. My best friend and I were sitting together. An upperclassman came over to our seat and asked my friend to sit with him. She did. He started giving her some light kisses and she responded. It wasn't long until his kisses weren't light anymore and his hands were very busy.

Another guy came to sit by me. All the way home he tried to kiss me but I wouldn't let him. He had never even spoken to me at school, so there was no way I was going to let him kiss me.

I worried a lot about my friend after that night. She had allowed herself to be put into a bad situation, and she didn't know how to get out of it. She probably hadn't been told how quickly a guy's sexual feelings could wake up. Two years later she got pregnant (not by the bus boy) and married before she finished school.

Avoid doing things that will put you in a situation that will be difficult to get out of. Remember, a little physical contact can go a long way.

Boys Are Afraid of Being Rejected by Girls

Ron wanted to date a beautiful girl who had just enrolled in his school, but he was afraid she would turn him down since she didn't know him. He told his friends that if they'd ask some girls out on a date, he'd ask the new girl out and they could triple date. They took him up on his plan.

They drove him to the girl's house so he could ask her out. When they got there, though, he wouldn't get out of the car. He told them to drive around the block one more time and he'd get out. They did. Then he said, "Go around one more time and I promise I'll get out." When they got to her house the third time, he still wouldn't budge. He told his friends he knew she would turn him down.

His two friends jumped out of the car, grabbed him, dragged him out, dumped him on the girl's sidewalk, and drove away. All he could do was go to the door and ask her out. She said yes, and both of them had a great time.

It may be hard for you to believe that boys are as afraid of saying the wrong thing or looking dumb or being embarrassed as you are. So give them a break! They're still learning how to ask girls for dates, so treat them the same way you would like to be treated.

What Guys Wish Girls Knew about Guys

"All boys aren't alike."

"I'm fun to be with. Give me a chance."

"I don't know how to express myself around girls."

"I'm not as stupid and dumb as I act in class."

"I'm afraid girls don't like me."

"I'm not the airhead I act like I am."

"Guys don't like to be put down."

"It hurts when a girl leads me on."

"If a guy breaks up with a girl, it doesn't mean he hates her."

"Guys have feelings, too."

Girl Facts

Girls have different feelings about boys than boys have about girls. There's no way a girl can dissect a boy's brain and see how he feels about girls. A girl only knows how she feels about boys. Here are some facts about what goes on inside of girls where guys are concerned.

Girls Talk Differently about Guys than Guys Talk about Girls

It doesn't wake up a girl's sexual feelings when she talks to her best friend or with a group of girls about her feelings for certain boys, or how she plans to get them to notice her, or how she feels when they fall for her plan. Girls just think it's fun to talk about boys.

Girls' Sexual Feelings Take Longer to Wake Up than Boys' Feelings Do

Although it may take a girl's sexual feelings longer to wake up than a boy's, it is very difficult for her to control those feelings once they are awake. When a girl lets a boy touch her exposed shoulders, her exposed or unexposed thighs, her breasts or genital area, it can lead to more than either of them can handle.

I went to a movie theater one evening where I noticed a couple sitting across the aisle from me. I knew the girl from my ninth grade class. She was shy and had a great shape. The boy looked older than she. He had his arm around her shoulders. When the theater lights were turned down and the movie started, I glanced at the couple again, and he had moved his arm so that he could touch her breast. No one had ever told me that it was wrong to let a boy touch certain parts of my body, but it looked wrong. Several days later I heard that the girl had become a "regular name" in the boys' locker room.

One Christian family counselor warns that some guys will try to push a girl's limits to see how far she will let them go. This is one way some boys test their authority with girls. Some will try to go all the way. When that happens, girls suffer the most, not only from fear of an unwanted pregnancy, but from the guilt of "letting it happen" or from losing status with their friends.

Say to yourself regularly, "I will not . . . repeat . . . I will *not* be a boy's 'conquest' and have my name become the main subject of locker-room conversation."

Consider the following: "If you must choose, take a good name rather than great riches; for to be held in loving esteem is better than silver and gold" (Proverbs 22:1). Say the names of some of your classmates. What's the first thing that pops into your mind when you say each name? When someone says *your* name, what do you want them to think about you?

You can't get away from your name. It sticks on tight. It won't let loose. A good name has a big price tag on it because it makes you a winner. A good name can mean approval and acceptance from your peers; it can bring you all kinds of great friendships. Another verse says, "A good reputation is more valuable than the most expensive perfume" (Ecclesiastes 7:1). A good reputation can give you more than if you were the richest person in the world!

Girls' Bodies Were Designed to Ovulate

Ovulation happens when, in the middle of your menstrual cycle, one of your egg cells is released from your ovary. To find out when this happens, start counting from the first day you menstruate. On the thirteenth, fourteenth, or fifteenth day, you will ovulate. Ovulation can cause girls to have very strong sexual feelings toward boys.

Keep in touch with this special part of your design by creating a secret code on your calendar, watching to see if your feelings for or about boys are greater during those days. Keeping track of your ovulation time is a good habit, and very helpful when you get into serious solo dating.

Many girls, especially those who have never been told how ovulation affects their emotions, give in to their strong sexual feelings and to the desires and pressure of guys. When things go beyond kissing and petting, boys and girls begin to experiment with the sexual parts of their bodies—

parts that are very sensitive to touch. When things go this far, their feelings get out of control and couples end up having sexual intercourse. (Sexual intercourse takes place when the male's penis is inserted into the female's vagina. The seminal fluid which holds the male's sperm cells is then released through his penis into the female's vagina. *If a male sperm unites with a female's egg cell, which is present when a girl ovulates, she becomes pregnant.*)

Creating romantic situations with a guy sounds exciting. But the end result usually isn't as great as a girl might think — especially when she may end up getting pregnant, her future changed by an on-the-spot choice.

Girls Love Being Treated Like They're Special

Being singled out by a guy who likes you and treats you like you're special can give you one of the greatest feelings in the world. One of the most beautiful love stories in the Scriptures is in the book of Song of Solomon. It describes the feelings of King Solomon as he singled out a woman he loved more than any other woman:

> *O most beautiful woman in all the world . . . How lovely your cheeks are, with your hair falling down upon them! . . . My beloved is a bouquet of flowers . . . Your eyes are those of doves . . . your teeth are white as sheep's wool . . . perfectly matched . . . your lips are like a thread of scarlet — and how beautiful your mouth. . . . you have ravished my heart, my lovely one, my bride . . . I am overcome by one glance of your eyes . . . How sweet is your love, my darling . . . You are like a lovely orchard bearing precious fruit, with the rarest of perfumes . . . You are a garden fountain, a well of living water, refreshing as the streams . . . how you capture my heart . . . you, my dove, my perfect one are . . .* without an equal! *(emphasis added)*

You may want to read the entire book of Song of Solomon. It makes a great love story. It lets you in on the normal and good feelings a man and a woman can have for each other.

The best part of this story is that King Solomon's bride felt the same about the king as he felt for her. Their kind of love was caring, warm, and passionate. It was nothing like the destructive kind of "love" that tries to force you to do something you shouldn't (like have sex before marriage).

My daughter Pam shared an equally beautiful love story. Her story expresses many of the feelings of rejection and insecurities she experienced in junior high—until she found her perfect guy, who was *"without an equal."*

"I remember the pain and how awkward I felt in the seventh to ninth grades as I tried to fit into the 'rich and popular' crowd. There were only two boys who were taller than me, so those were the two I hoped would like me. Unfortunately, they liked short, well-built girls. I was self-conscious and shy around boys. I don't remember ever being asked to dance at the parties.

"I was very aware of my appearance. I would take hours to do my makeup, hair, and nails, and to select just the right outfit. I picked out an outfit each night and painted my nails to match.

"Then came the tenth grade. I thanked God for that year. There were *lots* of boys taller than me. I stopped trying to fit into the old crowd. Soon I was welcomed and accepted by a less popular but more fun group. I made some great girl friends and that was good for me. My confidence grew by leaps and bounds. One of my friends set me up on a few dates and then I began to assert myself more around boys. That was fun! I realized they were just as insecure as I was.

"When I entered twelfth grade, I met Nelson. After many hours of group dates, double dates, and solo dates, I knew I'd found my Perfect 10."

(Four years after Pam and Nelson met, they got married, and now they're living "happily ever after.")

Every girl goes through times of feeling lonely, rejected, or unlovable. If you're going through this right now, hang on! Better days (and friends) are coming.

When you are struggling with a down time, remember the following Words and cheer up: "For I know the plans I have for you, says the Lord. They are plans for good . . . to give you a future and a hope" (Jeremiah 29:11).

The New Feelings Girls Have for Boys Are Normal!

After God made a man and a woman he "looked over all that he had made, and it was *excellent* in every way" (Genesis 1:31).

In the beginning, God rated everything he made as a Perfect 10. He created you, all of you, including the feelings you have (or will have) about boys. Those feelings were included in what he called "excellent in every way." *The Amplified Bible* says they are "suitable, pleasant—and [God] approved [them] completely" (Genesis 1:31).

The only time your feelings aren't "suitable" is when they get out of control. Ask God to help you make right relationships with the right kind of guys, and to keep your feelings and relationships "suitable," "good," and "excellent."

Doing this isn't easy, as one ninth grade girl and her boyfriend found out. They had to make a painful, but "excellent" choice in their relationship: "We both flirted around with each other for a long time. Finally we started going together. Then we got serious, too serious. I was afraid he wanted us to have sex. So we decided to break up. I still love him and I hurt a lot because I miss him. But we weren't ready for things to get that serious."

God knows how hard it is to keep your feelings and relationships under control. So he has given you these Words to encourage you: "The Lord is good and glad to teach the proper path to [you] . . . he will teach the ways that are right and best [he'll even let you know which guys are right for you] to those who humbly turn to him. And when [you] obey him, every path he guides [you] on is fragrant with his loving-kindness and his truth" (Psalm 25:8-10).

Think Tank
It's almost guaranteed: Someday some guy will try to talk you into having sexual intercourse with him. To help you be prepared for this, here are some common "reasons" you may hear for having premarital sex . . . and some great responses you can think about using:

Him: "If you won't go all the way with me, we might as well stop seeing each other."

My response: "It's been nice."

Your response:

Him: "Hey! We'll play it safe! What's the problem?"

My response: "There's no such thing as 100 percent safe with sex. I don't want to risk having a baby I'm not ready to be responsible for right now."

Your response:

Him: "If you loved me, you'd do it with me."

My response: "If you loved me, you wouldn't ask me to do it with you."

Your response:

Him: "Everybody else is doing it, why shouldn't we?"

My response: "I'm not 'everybody else'."

Your response:

Him: "We've said we love each other, so what's wrong with doing it?"

My response: "Prove it's right. Besides, we can love each other without having sex."

Your response:

Him: "I love you so much. There's nothing better you could do for me that would let me know how much you really love me."

My response: "I'm sure I could think of *something* better."

Your response:

"I've Already Done It!"

There are many junior high girls who have already had intercourse. For some girls, it felt good to be loved in that way. They liked being held close — it made them feel special. Other girls didn't want to have sex, but their friends talked them into it, or they didn't want to be the *only one* who hadn't done it, or they felt awkward telling the guy no. Some girls are afraid of losing their boyfriends if they don't give in.

After having sex, some girls said they hated the guys for talking them into it. Several said they really didn't like the guys they'd had sex with all that much or that it didn't give them the great feeling they thought they'd have. Many girls expressed anger, both with the guys and with themselves.

If you've had intercourse with a guy, you may be struggling with a lot of emotions. You may even hate yourself for participating in such an intimate act of love that was designed for couples who are committed to each other in marriage.

It's true that God did not design sex to be used outside of marriage. It is also true that God loves you and there is nothing you can do that is too terrible for him to forgive! Tell him you made a wrong choice. He will forgive you and he will help you change that part of your life.

Maybe it's time for you to start building a brand new reputation by saying no to guys. (This probably will be very difficult, but you *can* do it!) Guys who ask you to have sex with them don't even deserve an explanation for the change in you. Remember, you are responsible for the way you treat your body now. Saying no to sex is *your* choice.

Don't worry if your decision to say no to sex results in your having fewer dates. Instead of feeling bad or rejected, remind yourself that you've made a great choice: You're taking control of your body and treating it as something special.

These Words hold a special promise to help you stick to your decision. Memorize them and repeat them regularly while you're dating.

> *But remember this — the wrong desires that come into your life [desiring to have sexual intercourse] aren't anything new and different. Many others [maybe even a friend or a relative] have faced exactly the same problems before you. And* no temptation is irresistible. *You can trust God to keep the temptation from becoming so strong that you can't stand up against it, for he has promised this and will do what he says. He will show you how to escape temptation's power so that you can bear up patiently against it. (1 Corinthians 10:13, emphasis added)*

Girl and *Boy Facts*

You're not the first girl to make eye contact with a certain guy and have your heart thump so hard and fast that you were afraid people could see it jumping around. Adam and Eve's hearts probably did it the first time they saw each other. As hard as it may be to believe, I bet good old Mom and Dad had this heart condition when *they* were in junior high!

With all these feelings and hormones flying around, some difficult and painful things will happen. The most painful part of boy and girl relationships is breaking up. You'll probably go through some painful breakups before you find your Perfect 10 guy.

It's great when girls and guys can be sensitive to each

other's new feelings. When they learn to control their new feelings, they're letting each other know, "Hey! You're really special and I'm going to keep you that way."

These Words tell you how special both of you are: "Thank you [God] for making me so wonderfully complex! [Even when I can't understand the feelings I'm having!] It is amazing to think about. Your workmanship is marvelous . . . How precious it is, Lord, to realize that you are thinking about me constantly [even when I'm on a date with a special guy]! I can't even count how many times a day your thoughts turn towards me. And when I waken in the morning, you are still thinking of me!" (Psalm 139:14-18).

You are so special that God chose you to be the "temple" where he lives: "Haven't you yet learned that your body is the home of the Holy Spirit God gave you, and that he lives within you?" (1 Corinthians 6:19).

It's important to keep your body special for the young man who will someday pass the test to be your husband. It's even more important to do so because your body is the place where God, your designer, has chosen to live.

Since you're so special to God, he has a wonderful plan for you. "The Lord will work out his plans for [your] life — for [his] loving-kindness continues forever" (Psalm 138:8). Part of his plan for you includes boys. Finding the right boy for you will take going to house parties, then group dates, then double dates, and finally solo dates. Special relationships with boys will bring out all kinds of feelings: friendship, excitement, rejection, jealousy, heartbreak, happiness, sadness, loneliness, anger, and love.

All of these feelings, and a million others, are normal. They are a part of the formula for eventually finding the guy that's right for you. Be patient. Enjoy the search! If you'll let yourself, you will have some great years observing and getting to know these interesting, hard-to-understand, two-legged male creatures!

House Party Games

Here are some great games for you to try at your house parties. Read over all of them, then decide which ones would work best for the kids you have invited to your party. Don't use all of them at once. Save some for a future party. The first two are especially good for getting everyone loosened up and involved.

Whichever games you decide to play, be sure you stop each one while everyone is still having fun with it. Keeping a game going too long is one of the fastest ways to ruin it.

Sit Down If . . .

This game really helps a group get to know each other well! Have everyone stand up, then tell them that if what you say fits them, they should sit down.

Start: "Sit down if . . ."

You sing in the shower.
Your belly button is an "outtie."
You didn't use deodorant today.
You've worn the same socks two days in a row.
You kiss with your eyes open.
You use hairspray.
You haven't taken a shower this week.
Your eyes are green.
You like liver.
You are a girl and you didn't shave your legs today.
You are a guy and you *did* shave your legs today.
You sucked your thumb as a kid.
You still suck your thumb.
Your nose is runny and you don't have any Kleenex.
Your mother picks out your clothes.

You can add to this list of things to say. Once you've gone through your list, if someone is still standing, make up a few more items to see if you can get them to sit down. (For example, "Sit down if you have white socks on," or ". . . if you're in love," and so on). If you've run out of items and someone is *still* standing, say, "Everyone who is sitting down is normal. We hope the rest of you will be normal some day soon!"

Circles of . . .

This game is a great way to get a party going. You need an even number of people (at least fourteen to twenty) to play this.

Have everyone start walking around the room. Then yell, "Make circles of three and kneel!" Everyone must run and kneel together in a circle with the number of people you have chosen. If some don't make it to a group, that's OK. They can still keep playing. Let the group talk for a few minutes, then yell, "Break up!" Everyone should start walking around again. After a few seconds, yell, "Make circles of . . .," choosing whatever number you want. Do this several times.

For the last round, count silently how many you have in your group, then divide that number by two. Then yell, "Make circles of . . .," using the number that will divide the group in half. (For example, if you have twenty people, say, "Make circles of ten.")

Be sure you keep this game fast paced.

Scavenger Hunt

Make up a list before the party of things that are usually found in purses and billfolds (e.g., gum, brushes, money, pictures, combs, paper clips, movie ticket stubs, candy, etc.). Have everyone get their purses or billfolds, then divide the group into teams.

Each team will send one of its people to a leader in the center of the room. This leader will then whisper the name of an object from your list into the person's ear. The person will return to his group and *pantomime* the object until someone in the group guesses what it is. (Tell the groups to talk softly so that the other groups won't hear their guesses.) When the object is guessed, have everyone look in their purses and billfolds to find it and get it to the leader in the center of the room. The first person to get there with the item wins that round. Then each group chooses another representative and repeats the process until all the items on the list have been found.

You may want to give a stick of gum or some other small prize to the members of the group that wins.

Birdie on a Perch

Have boys and girls pair up. Then form two circles, boys on the outside and girls on the inside, facing their partners. Don't have any more than eight couples in each circle.

Choose some kind of signal (a whistle, a duck call, some kind of bell, etc.). When you give the signal, the boys should start walking counter-clockwise, and the girls should start walking clockwise. After a few seconds, sound the signal again. When you do so, the boys are to squat down with one knee on the floor. At the same time, each girl should run to her partner and sit on his knee. The last couple to get the "birdie on the perch" is out. Keep the game going until only one couple is left.

You might want to give a sack of birdseed or a small toy bird to the winning couple.

Footsigning

Form groups of five boys. Have them take off one shoe and sock. Each guy has three minutes to get as many girls as possible to sign one foot. Each girl can only sign four feet!

You may want to give a pair of clean (or dirty) socks to the winners from each group.

Mummy Wrap

Form teams of two couples. Give each team a roll of toilet paper. One person has to be the "mummy." The object is to wrap the mummy from head to toe, without letting any part of the body show. The couple who has the best-wrapped mummy wins.

You may want to give the winner an unused roll of toilet paper.

Another version: Have each couple wrap themselves.

Wet a Way to Go

Choose three couples. Have the boys lie on the floor (it's best if you have an old blanket or a plastic tarp under them). Place an empty plastic soda bottle on each boy's forehead. They can hold them in place. Then give each of the three girls a bowl of water and a sponge, telling them to fill the bottles with water squeezed from the sponge.

Prize for the winning couple: Two "real" sodas.

Another version: Blindfold the girls and have them each pour a cup of water into the bottle (which is on her partner's forehead, as before). The one who gets the most water in the bottle wins.

Unusual Banana Splits

Have the boys lie on their backs and have the girls "build" banana splits in the boys' wide-open mouths (they should be careful, however, not to choke the boys!). Be sure to take pictures of these creations.

Refreshment ideas: If you decide to play this game, have your guests each bring an item that goes with banana splits (or have each person bring a banana, and you provide the toppings). Set these items out when the game is finished and let everybody build a banana split (in a bowl).

Ping-Pong Hockey

You will need Ping-Pong balls, three empty one-pound coffee cans, and straws.

Divide into teams, with no more than six to eight people on a team. Give everyone a straw, and draw an imaginary starting line. Lay the coffee cans on their sides about twenty feet from the starting line. Then have the teams line up single file and give the first person a Ping-Pong ball. That person must get down on his knees, place the Ping-Pong ball on the floor, then use the straw to blow the ball into the can. When this has been done, the person grabs the ball and runs it back to the next person in line. Each member must take a turn blowing the ball into the can. The first team done wins.

Freezer Burn

You'll need three couples, three bowls of ice cream, six spoons, and six blindfolds. Sit the couples at a table with their ice cream, then blindfold them. When you say, "Go!" the couples are to feed each other ice cream from their bowl. The first couple to empty the bowl wins.

A fun way to serve refreshments when you play this game is to find some old manual ice cream makers. Divide the group into as many teams as you have ice cream makers, then see which team can get their ice cream frozen first. This takes lots of energy, but it's great fun!

I've Never

You'll need a small sack of macaroni or beans.

Have the group sit in a large circle. The first person starts by completing the phrase "I've never . . ." with something he or she has never done. (Examples: "gone skiing," "scuba dived," "gotten an 'A' in math.") Players should say things that both boys and girls will be able to relate to.

Anyone else in the circle who hasn't done what the person says takes a bean or piece of macaroni. Proceed around the circle, having each person complete the phrase with something he or she has never done, and having anyone else who hasn't done that thing take a bean or a piece of macaroni.

The person with the fewest beans or pieces of macaroni at the end of the game wins.

A bag of beans or a box of macaroni might be a good prize for the winner. Or you could collect the beans or macaroni from the group and present them to the winner in the original bag or box.

Other Games

Table games are great for house parties. You might ask each of your guests to bring a favorite, so long as it is something that both boys and girls can play.

Some group favorites are Twister, Outburst, Pictionary (regular or Bible), Clue, Life, Generosity*, Monopoly, Parcheesi, Chinese Checkers, or Trivial Pursuit.

*Available from Tyndale House Publishers

FOUR

Secret Feelings about Friends

Dear Diary,
D.P. is my very best friend. She's so much fun to be around and is super-easy to talk to. We don't fight very often because we can talk things through. If she was ever dishonest with me or dumped me, I'd be very hurt!

Lindey

You probably can't remember when you didn't like being around other girls. When you were small — standing knee-deep in dolls, finger paints, and glue — you probably told your mom you were bored. Then you'd ask her to let you invite someone to come over and play with you. Playing was more fun when you had someone to play with.

As you got older, you and some other girls probably started running around together. Now you do everything and go everywhere together. You can be yourself around each other and no one in the group thinks you're weird. These girls are your "group" friends.

Once in awhile, certain school activities probably pull other girls into your life. You enjoy being with them. You'd like to get to know them better and do more things with them, but there never seems to be enough time. Even though you don't spend regular time together, you consider these girls your "part-time" friends.

While you're running around with several types of girls, one girl wins out over all the rest and she becomes your "best" friend.

Group Friends

Group friends are good friends who do all kinds of things together. Many situations bring them together — classes with impossible teachers, parents getting divorced, dealing with pests (in the form of brothers and sisters), boy problems.

There are many kinds of personalities within group friendships, but these girls usually have enough in common to make them like to be with each other. One of the group friends might be loud and another one quiet. One dates, the others don't. One can't sit still and another thinks being active means turning the pages of a magazine or turning the television on and off with a remote control. One excels in sports, another in music. One of the girls has a great sense of humor to balance the one who takes life too seriously.

When I started junior high there were five girls who were my group friends. A.G. laughed most of the time. H.M. was twelve inches shorter than I was (we had fun making crazy remarks to each other about our heights). H.M. laughed a lot, too. B.G. was two years older than the rest of us. When she started dating a certain guy, she told us what they did on their dates. (Her boyfriend would have died if he had known that she even told us how they kissed!) D.H. was the quiet one in our group, but she was still an important part of it. My sister and I completed the group.

Our group stood around our lockers before school and

talked. We stood together in the cafeteria lines, sat together in assemblies, and had classes together. We went to ball games together. We voted for each other at school elections.

It can take a while for the right personalities to mix as group friends. Girls drift in and out of different groups, searching for the one that fits their needs. No matter who they are, though, all girls want and need to be accepted by a group of friends.

Pam tried for two years to fit into a certain group of kids. She ached for them to accept her. They invited her to their parties but she never felt accepted. They were "all right" girls, but they weren't the right group for Pam. She needed a group that would give her a big dose of confidence. She needed to see that she was really a neat person and she didn't have to try to be someone other than who she was.

Later, Pam found a group that *was* right for her. Two of the girls introduced her to the other girls and they accepted her and gave her lots of positive strokes. When Pam found the right group friends, a whole new world opened up for her!

What Group Friends Do Best

Group friends scheme together to get a guy to like one of the girls in their group. They scream together when the guy starts falling for their friend. They scream *louder* when the guy gets up his nerve to ask their friend on a date.

Group friends keep telephone wires hot! No excuse is too small for one of them to call another on the phone. They call each other to make plans to go to ball games, to study, to shop, to gripe, to see what the others are wearing to school the next day, and to talk about boys. They beg their parents to let them have sleepovers every weekend. They work overtime on their school schedules so they can have classes together. Their teachers work overtime planning seating arrangements to keep group friends apart in class!

Your group friends tell you things that no one else will tell you. They don't hesitate to tell you your lipstick is smeared or globbed on your front teeth, there's something green hanging between your teeth, your blouse is unbuttoned, there's a big rip under your sleeve, or your bra strap is showing. They're honest when you ask them if a certain outfit looks good on you. They let you know when your slip is hanging three inches below your skirt, you have a run in your hose, catsup in the corner of your mouth, blanket fuzz in your hair, or mascara streaming down your cheek.

Read the following Words to get a clue as to what makes group friends:

A man that hath [group] friends, must show himself friendly. (Proverbs 18:24, KJV)

[A friend's] suggestions are as pleasant as perfume. (Proverbs 27:9)

Be beautiful inside. (1 Peter 3:4)

Group friends don't care what size or shape you come in—they see what you are on the inside (beautiful) as well as what you are on the outside (friendly and honest). That's what group friends like about each other.

Part-Time Friends

Part-time friends come and go in your life at special times. You sit across the room from them in class or close to them at ball games and school assemblies. You talk when you see each other in the halls and at shopping malls. There's something special between you even though you don't spend much time together.

M.W. was one of my part-time friends in junior high. For a long time, I thought she was better than me. Her dad owned the town theater. Her grandfather was the newspaper editor. She lived in a beautiful two-story house. She wore the kind of clothes to school that I saved to wear to church.

Once she asked me to spend the night with her. We talked and laughed almost all night. Those special hours sealed our friendship because we learned what it meant to accept, respect, and enjoy each other.

Some of your part-time friends may be school leaders. They get elected as class officers, cheerleaders, queens, newspaper and yearbook editors. They're voted "Most Popular" and "Most Likely to Succeed." You don't have regular contact with these friends, but you respect them for the way they handle their leadership roles. You know they won't walk down the halls after winning an election, checking off their "I'm More Important Than You" list, getting on the loudspeaker and telling everyone how important they are, or barely managing to squeak out a "hi" to anyone who is one step lower on the social scale than they are.

God uses all kinds of people to help work out the special plans he has for your life. Part-time friends fit into his plan. After you've known them for a while, some of the strong qualities you like in your part-time friends may start showing up in you.

Best Friends

A best friend is the friend you trust more than anyone else. You can tell her anything—even what boy you like—and you know she won't tell anyone. She's always there when you need her. (Not everyone has a best friend, of course. That's OK. Some people don't feel they need a best friend; they like having a variety of friends.)

"She's tuned into my feelings. She knows all my secrets and she's a great listener. She cares about me, I mean she really cares about me." Karen, 10th grade

My best friend was my sister Jackie. She and I were one year apart in age, so neither of us needed another best friend. We went almost everywhere together. We shared the same bedroom, enjoyed the same school activities, and talked together about many things. We were always there for each other.

It's a great feeling when you meet someone who likes you as much as you like her, and you are each other's best friend.

These Words describe what best friends do best!

A [best] friend . . . sticks closer than a brother. (Proverbs 18:24)

Two are better than one. . . . If one falls down, his friend can help him up. (Ecclesiastes 4:9-10, NIV)

The following old Jewish saying would be great to write and give to your best friend:

A faithful friend is a strong protection
A person who has found one has found a treasure
A faithful friend is beyond price and his value cannot be weighed
A faithful friend is life-giving medicine and those who fear the Lord will find it.

How Some Girls Feel about Best Friends

"If something hurts her it hurts me, too." Diana, 8th grade
"She builds me up when others put me down. When my mother died she hurt with me and we became better friends than ever." Terri, 9th grade

"Our friendship began when we were both feeling pretty lonely. So it only seemed natural that we should be best friends." Shanna, 10th grade

"We're inseparable. We have the same wacky sense of humor, the same personalities. We just 'click.' I admire her a lot." Tess, 8th grade

"We hated each other for a long time. Then one night we stayed all night with some other girls and we promised to try to get along with each other. We got to talking and we've been best friends since then." Debbie, 9th grade

"She was there for me when a guy really hurt me. She had set me up with him and then he dumped me. She was there for me because she felt really bad that she was the one that got us together. Now we're friends for life." Ariana, 10th grade

"We have some of the same problems." Janis, 7th grade

"We noticed how much we were alike and then we started hanging around together." Elena, 8th grade

When Best Friends Aren't Friends Anymore

It's a painful time when best friends stop being best friends. Sometimes girls don't know what went wrong, why the friendship ended. The breakup doesn't make sense. They had always hung out together at malls on Saturday afternoons, sunbathed and sunburned together during the summer—they had practically lived at each other's houses.

As long as they were best friends, each girl honestly believed she could handle anything: teasing from other kids, stupid nicknames, not having a date when everyone else had one, even days when everything went wrong. It didn't matter, because there was always someone to stand by her, someone who knew exactly what to say or do to make the other one feel better. After the breakup, the girls involved often dread going to school and seeing their friend with other friends, doing the same things they had done together.

> *"She meant so much to me. All I could*
> *think was, 'I'll never have a friend as good*
> *as her again.' I valued her friendship and I*
> *felt very lonely and lost for months."*
> Hannah, 10th grade

Any broken relationship hurts! If you ever have that kind of hurt, don't suffer alone. Talk with another friend or an older person you trust and who will listen. These people may not have answers for you, but talking about what happened will make you feel better.

It will take time, but eventually you will be able to look around and see that there are other girls who need a friend as badly as you do. When you start reaching out and developing new friendships, your hurts will start healing.

These Words will help you while you're hurting:

Rescue me [from this hurt] because you are the God who always does what is right. Answer quickly when I cry to you; bend low and hear my whispered plea. (Psalm 31:1-2)

[God] is a refuge for them in their times of trouble. He does not ignore the prayers of [people] in trouble when they call to him for help. (Psalm 9:9,12)

Give your [hurts] to the Lord. He will carry them. (Psalm 55:22)

Lord, when [hurts] fill my mind, when my heart is in turmoil, quiet me and give me renewed hope and cheer. (Psalm 94:19)

In my distress I prayed to the Lord and he answered me and rescued me. He is for me! How can I be afraid? What can mere man [or an ex-friend] do to me? The Lord is on my side, he will help me. (Psalm 118:5-7)

How Girls Feel about Losing a Best Friend

"She found a girl she thought she liked better and I'm not sure why. I felt very hurt." AnnMarie, 7th grade

"One day she walked into the room and started yelling at me. That really hurt because I didn't do anything to her. Now most of my friends have turned away from me." Elaine, 8th grade

"It makes me feel like I'll never be good friends with anyone again." Carla, 7th grade

"I started having stomach cramps. I still can't believe it happened. Sometimes I hate that person because of what she did to me. I've tried to write how I feel, but I really can't explain my feelings." Glenna, 9th grade

"When our friendship broke off I thought I could never tell anyone a secret again. I was afraid she would tell everyone some of the deepest secrets I had told her." Kathie, 8th grade

"She came first in my life. I felt betrayed in a way. I didn't understand what was going on. We kept getting farther and farther apart." Heidi, 8th grade

"I'm going through losing a best friend right now. I feel bitter, confused, and betrayed." Debbie, 7th grade

One More Girl Type

It would be great if every girl you knew fit into one of the three friend groups . . . but that doesn't happen. There's another "girl type," one that you avoid. These are the girls who do things that get you upset, or who do things you really don't like—girls who tease, make embarrassing remarks, or regularly put down other people.

I remember trying to do everything I could to avoid one certain girl. She *always* came up with remarks about my height. I even tried to find out what *she* was self-conscious about so I could embarrass her the way she embarrassed me — but I couldn't ever think of anything to say. My daughter Beth had some similar problems. One of her diary entries read: "S.E. is weird. She's always putting me down."

The worst part of it is that you know you'd get into trouble if you did what you felt like doing when these girl types make their remarks. Instead, you walk away, silently wishing a strong wind would come along and blow these girls to another school — or another planet — so you wouldn't have to see or hear them anymore.

You may find it impossible to believe you could ever respect, admire, or enjoy this girl type. It's even harder to believe that this girl might not be *trying* to make you feel miserable. But both of these things could be true.

It could be that a girl who constantly teases or puts others down is really saying, "Notice me," "Please don't leave me out," "Give me some of your attention." Maybe these girls have never had a best friend, group friends, or even part-time friends.

You don't spend lots of time around girls like this, but check out these Words. They may give you a hint that even these girls shouldn't be totally ignored or excluded: "Do you think you deserve credit for merely loving those who love you? . . . And if you do good only to those who do you good — is that so wonderful? . . . Try to show as much compassion as [God] does . . . Go easy on others; *then* they will do the same for you" (Luke 6:32-33, 36-37, emphasis added).

Pressures from Other Girls

One day in junior high my history teacher announced that we would have a true/false test the next day. She said she would read the statements and we would put our answers on paper. I didn't study for the test, but one of my friends did.

At recess, I told this friend about a plan I had: she could

give me the answers! If the answer was "true," she was to hold up one finger; if it was "false," two fingers. She really didn't want to do it, but I knew she would. I pressured her into it. She couldn't refuse because she was afraid I wouldn't be her friend anymore.

Many junior high girls have to face the pressure of doing whatever it takes to be accepted by others . . . like using bad language. There are a lot of four-letter words floating through the air in junior high. The kids who use them attract attention when they say them. It may be one of their last attempts to get someone to notice them. If that's what it takes, that's what they'll do.

> *"It seems like people keep forcing me to do things and it's hard for me to say no. I don't really want to do those things, but I don't want to lose my friends either."*
> Amy, 9th grade

In eighth grade I heard lots of boys, especially the "popular" boys, saying God's name as a swear word. I knew this was wrong—especially since my teacher at church had told us God himself said it was wrong! "You shall not use the name of Jehovah your God irreverently [lightly or as a swear word] nor use it to swear to a falsehood. You will not escape punishment if you do" (Exodus 20:7).

I wasn't sure what the punishment would be if I used God's name like that, but that verse scared me. But even though that verse sounded true while I was at church, I honestly believed that if the popular kids used God's name like that, it couldn't be all that terrible.

One day at recess I was playing catch with another girl. She threw the ball to me and I missed it. As I was running after it, I yelled, "G——, Betty, can't you throw any better than that?" I said it loudly, so some of the other kids could hear me. As soon as the word *God* left my mouth, I was sure

God was going to punish me by striking me dead before recess was over! I felt terrible. I'd had no idea that doing something God had told me not to do would make me feel so awful.

No one else had pressured me to say what I'd said. *I* had pressured myself. I thought that I would be more accepted by the "in" group if I used their kind of language.

I still remember what my Sunday school teacher, Mrs. Goodwin, said once when some of us had asked her what made people use bad language: "The reason people use bad language is because they have such a limited vocabulary that they can't find any other words to express what they want to say."

> *"Some pressures are overdramatized, but I feel pressured because I get pushed from all directions and don't know where to go."* Alyce, 8th grade

Another common pressure junior high kids face is smoking. P.F. was one of my friends in eighth grade. One day while I was at her house and her parents were gone, we went into her bedroom and she closed the door. She opened a small wooden box and took out a package of cigarettes. She took a cigarette from the package and started smoking it. She asked me if I'd like to smoke. I said no (I didn't want her to know I didn't know how to smoke).

A few days later I took a cigarette I'd found and some matches and went downstairs to the darkest corner of our basement. I tried to hold the cigarette between my two fingers the way P.F. had held hers. My fingers felt numb. I put the cigarette in my mouth and sucked in. Every time I took a short puff I got a strange feeling in my stomach. Even worse than that was the fear that Mom and Dad might get off work early and catch me. I didn't finish the cigarette, but I hid the evidence and prayed that Mom and Dad wouldn't smell the smoke when they got home.

My first smoking attempt and the way I felt during and after it helped me decide I didn't want to ever smoke another cigarette. I sure didn't want to spend any more time alone with P.F. No one ever asked me to smoke again, but if someone had, I would've said no.

If you're struggling with whether or not to smoke, the warnings from cigarette packages may help you make your decision. They read, "Surgeon General's Warning: Quitting smoking now greatly reduces serious risks to your health," and "Smoking by pregnant women may result in fetal injury, premature birth, and low birth weight."

These Words may also help you say no to smoking (and to drinking and drugs):

> *Has anyone ever told you that your body is the temple where God lives? Don't put anything into your body that would pollute it and keep you from bringing honor to God and to the 'temple' where he lives. (Author's paraphrase of 1 Corinthians 6:19-20)*

There are some other, less obvious pressures, too. I remember facing one of those pressures when I was in the eighth grade. A new boy enrolled in our school. He had dark, greasy hair that hung in his eyes. He wore faded jeans, old plaid shirts, and big, dirty shoes. The one thing he had going for him was that he made good grades.

Some of us got together and told our teacher that this boy smelled bad and we didn't want to sit close to him. The next day she moved him to the back of the room. I wish the teacher had checked out our story. He *didn't* smell. He only looked like he did. I've never forgotten how he must have felt when we didn't accept him.

The pressure to like only people who *we* think are acceptable is everywhere. Too many people have the habit of deciding, from the minute new students walk into the room, whether or not they are going to accept them. One seventh grade girl commented, "I feel pressured to let my friends make up my mind for me." Another girl said, "One of the pressures I've felt is people choosing my friends. If they don't like a person they will tell me lies about that person to break up any friendship we may have."

There are lots of reasons people use for not accepting someone: they dress differently, talk differently, are a different race, have speech problems, have trouble learning, have a physical handicap, hold different religious beliefs . . . the list is endless. You'll always be around people who are different from you. But no matter who the person is, the two of you will always have two things in common: (1) Everyone has feelings, and (2) Everyone has a deep need to be accepted.

The following poem was written by a tenth grade girl soon after she moved to a different school. It proves how badly a person needs to be accepted.

The Wall Around Me

There's a wall around me,
    and I can't break through.
Although I try to climb it,
    I fail each time I do.
No one hears me crying,
    Darkness all around.
There seems to be no end to it,
    the pain goes on and on.
Each brick is lined
    with something that I fear.
"Isolation" its foundation,
    "loneliness" marks each tier.
A new row is added
    day by day by day.

Getting high and higher and higher still,
   I cannot get away.
There's a wall around me,
   and I can't break through.
Although I try to climb it,
   I fail each time I do.
(J.C.S.)

There's a great way to say no to the pressure to not like someone: *Pretend you're that person for one day.* While you're doing that, hang onto these Words: "[Treat] others [the way] you want them to [treat] you" (Matthew 7:12). This verse can change the way you treat people every time.

Another pressure many girls face is the pressure to have a boyfriend. Sometimes girls feel there's something wrong with them if they can't get a guy to like them. Some girls have felt so much pressure in this area that they pretend to like a certain guy, hoping this will get them into the "right" group. Other girls feel pressured to do what guys want them to do, even when they don't want to do it. Some girls feel pressured to kiss on the first date, hold hands, make out, or let a boy hang all over them at school.

One of the most difficult and serious pressures is the pressure to have sex. A ninth grade girl said on her questionnaire, "Society is enforcing it. I don't do it, but if you want to be 'in' you almost have to." Girls who give in to this pressure discover too late that there is no good reason to have premarital sex. One tenth grade girl wrote: "I feel depressed and disappointed in myself. I get pressured to do it. I feel like hurting myself for doing it afterwards, because it's wrong." (Chapter three gives you some great information and tips on dealing with this pressure. When you face pressures in this area—or even *before* you face them—turn back to chapter three and read it over carefully.)

Other Pressures

Here are several common areas where girls feel pressured.

Wearing Makeup

"One of my friends in fifth grade tried to get me to wear makeup, but my parents told me I couldn't wear it yet. My friend figured a way I could put on makeup after I got to school and take it off before I went home. I didn't do it. I would've felt guilty and I loved my parents too much to do that." Michelle, 7th grade

Wearing Certain Clothes

"I feel pressured to have certain friends and wear certain clothes. I have to stay looking good. It seems like someone always has to be better!" Janelle, 8th grade

Listening to Hard Rock Music

"I feel pressured to listen to hard rock and I don't even like it!" Nancy, 9th grade

Saying No To Pressure

A seventh grade girl asked me if I ever feel pressure from other people to do things I know is wrong. I told her yes. I may not have the same kind of pressures she has, but I *do* have them. Everyone does. We have to constantly decide how we're going to handle pressures.

As hard as it may be to believe, all pressure isn't bad. Pressure can be good when you give yourself time to think about the consequences for giving in, then make the right decision.

Not doing something because you're afraid you'll get caught isn't all bad. Maybe that will keep you from being pushed into doing things you know aren't right for you. One night when Dana was at a party she got some pressure from the group to do something she knew was wrong. She told us later that when she was being pressured, her dad's and my faces flashed in her mind. She knew how we would feel if we ever found out she had given in and done what she was being pressured to do. She said no.

Think back to when you were about two years old and still trying to figure out how to keep peas from falling out of your baby spoon. This was about the same time you were into saying "No!"

You practiced saying no every day. When your mother picked you up from your crib each morning and started to take off your pajamas, you pulled away, clenched your chubby little fists and said, "No." (Translation: "I don't *want* to change clothes. It feels like you're jerking off my ears when you pull my pajama top over my head.")

At mealtime, your mother told you to stop throwing your spaghetti on the floor. As you were swinging your spoon around and the spaghetti was flying in midair, hanging on the walls and sliding down the windows, you said, "No!"

Your dad told you to stop turning off the television or to stop standing in front of it. You said, "No!"

No was such an easy word to say until you got to fifth and sixth grade. Have you figured out *why* it's harder to say no now than when you were small? It's probably because you really want kids to like you. You're afraid that if you say no and don't go along with what other kids are doing (or what they're trying to get you to do), they may decide they don't like you! That's a big risk.

Girls Who've Said No to Pressures

"I keep telling myself, 'I *won't* give in when I know something is wrong." Vicki, 8th grade

"I've decided I'm one person. I can't be like my friends and other kids my age." Krystal, 9th grade

"I know I'm different because I don't use bad language or have my mind on sex all the time. I don't pick on other kids who do but I stand by what I believe is right." Jane, 9th grade

"I believe in myself, not in what someone else pressures me to be." Ann, 8th grade

Dana got into a bad situation when she was in ninth grade. She wanted to be accepted by a certain group of girls so badly that when she was invited to pledge their sorority, she couldn't say no. The sorority wasn't school sponsored so the members were free to make their own rules.

The verbal abuse the members gave the pledges (the girls who were picked to *possibly* be in the sorority) was terrible. They screamed at the pledges and verbally abused them until they were voted in . . . *if* they were voted in. The pledges couldn't say no to what they were being told to do because they wanted to be accepted into the group.

No matter what your friends try to pressure you to do . . . no matter what messages you're getting from the Top Forty love songs . . . no matter what some of the dumb television programming tries to get you to believe, God gives you some Words that are great to hang onto when the pressure's on!

Remember this — the wrong desires that come into your life [cursing, smoking, excluding someone, cheating, lying, drinking, taking drugs, having sex, etc.] aren't anything new and different. Many others have faced exactly the same [pressures] before you. And no [pressure] is irresistible. You can trust God to keep the [pressure] from becoming so strong that you can't stand up against it, for he has promised this and will do what he says. He will show you how to escape [the power of pressure] so that you can bear up patiently against it. (1 Corinthians 10:13, emphasis added)

What Senior High Girls Think about Pressure

"Things I'm pressured about now can have a greater, more dangerous effect on life." Gloria, 11th grade

"When I was twelve, I was pressured with kissing, hugging, and holding hands with a guy; throwing paper wads at teachers; and cursing. Now I'm pressured with drugs, drinking, smoking and sex." Sharon, 11th grade

"I'm not as easily influenced by kids my age as I was when I was in junior high. I'm more my own person now and I don't feel like I have to be just like everyone else anymore." Erin, 12th grade

FIVE

Secret
Feelings
about
Teachers

Dear Diary:
Today when I was hurting, Mrs. S. came to me and tried
to help. She just sat and listened because she knew I
needed someone to talk to. Mary told me Mrs. S. never
gives anyone any help. She said Mrs. S. treated everyone
like pond scum. I thought she was kind of nice.

Lindey

Teachers are different! They have eyes in the back of their heads. I should have remembered that fact when I tried to cheat on a test in fifth grade. I didn't know my teacher, Miss Jessie, saw me until I got the test back with this note on it: "You got an 'F' for cheating."

The next day the teacher made me apologize to the class for cheating. I had other chances to cheat after that, but after the pain and embarrassment I experienced that first time I knew cheating wasn't worth it.

I still liked Miss Jessie, even after she made me apologize. I think I know why: She didn't have any "pets." She was fair to all her students. She treated me like she would have treated any other student who cheated. She would've broken her record for being fair if she had let me get by with what I'd done. Miss Jessie was one of my Type A teachers.

Teacher Types

Once upon a time *all* teachers were junior high kids. They passed notes in class; flirted; got embarrassed, yelled at, and laughed at; made failing grades and mistakes; were self-conscious; had problems at home; had teachers they liked and teachers they didn't like. Then they grew up and became the teachers kids liked or didn't like.

Maybe it would help you understand your feelings about teachers if you learned why some are easy — and others almost impossible — to get along with. (You might want to encourage your teachers to read this chapter, too, so they can learn about some of the secret feelings girls have about them.)

There are two types of teachers: Type A and Type B. You probably like Type A teachers instantly. You'd probably move out of your house and call school "home" if you had all Type A teachers.

Don't start packing yet. Once you moved in you'd find out that you'd be living with some Type B teachers, too. You will have this type of teacher at least a few times during your first twelve years of school. These are the teachers who give you so many problems you've wondered why they ever wanted to be teachers!

Type A Teachers

Word gets around fast about Type A teachers. You want to be in their classes. You may not like the subjects they teach, but you make good grades in their classes because you like the way they teach and the way they treat their students. You get the feeling these teachers know you're human; they understand that you get hungry, or have trouble sitting still, or have personal problems. They know you come complete with feelings. They stay after school to help you with assignments until your mind clicks and you stop saying, "I *still* don't understand."

You know they spend hours preparing for classes because they present the subjects in interesting and creative ways. There are even history teachers in the Type A category. Most people would think you were crazy if you ran over people in the halls between classes to get a front seat in your history class . . . until they found out you had a Type A history teacher. Before you had that teacher, you believed that each page of your history book had the word *boring* written in the upper right hand corner. A Type A teacher can make even history come alive.

Beth had a Type A history teacher. This woman always found extra historical facts to share with her class. The more far-out the information, the more Beth liked it. She would come home from school and tell us what she had learned. I *never* listened that closely or enjoyed history that much when I was in junior high!

It's like that in any class with a Type A teacher. If you have trouble with math, Type A teachers encourage you to keep trying even though you still count on your fingers to find the answers. Type A English teachers know you'll eventually master the English language, even though you're trying to understand what split infinitives and dangling participles are. They hang in there with you when your spelling looks like it was written in Russian or Pig Latin. Your Type A science teachers believe that some day you *will* find what you've been assigned to find under the microscope.

You trust Type A teachers. You hang around after school to talk to them about problems you wouldn't talk about with anyone else. You know they will listen and give good advice if you ask them for it. They understand that having boy problems, trouble at home, or being sick can affect the way you act and learn.

What Girls Say about Type A Teachers

"She doesn't teach the class the same old way." Erin, 8th grade

"She is realistic and has a good sense of humor." Angela, 10th grade

"I've been going through a hard time with my parents and Mrs. P. told me if I ever needed anyone to talk to she was there. She notices if I'm in a bad mood or upset. It just seems like she's really tuned into my feelings. Most of all, she really acts like she cares. I can tell." Allyssa, 9th grade

"She makes our class work really hard, but somehow she makes it fun." Jackie, 9th grade

"She explains things over and over until everybody understands. I like that in a teacher." Laurel, 8th grade

"When she found out a friend of mine died, she talked to me and shared my sorrow." Lauren, 7th grade

"She helps when I'm down because she really knows how I feel. She really cares about what happens to us and I love her to death." Renae, 8th grade

"She's more than a teacher. She's a friend. She shares her feelings toward us and she lets us voice ours, too." Cherise, 10th grade

"She keeps discipline but is still friendly. I talk to her about my family problems and my boyfriends and she really gives me good advice." Merri, 9th grade

Mr. H. was one of Dana's Type A English teachers. In the middle of the school year, Dana broke up with her boyfriend. She had a rough time getting over the breakup. I talked with her and, after she said it was OK for me to do it, I called Mr. H. I told him Dana had to be absent from class, and I told him *why*. I had to call him several times when

Dana couldn't face coming to class. Dana was hurting and Mr. H understood. He's still her favorite teacher because of the way he responded to her struggle.

Type A teachers are able to say, "I'm sorry," "I was wrong," "I don't know the answer." These Words from Proverbs 15:2 describe Type A teachers: "A wise teacher makes learning a joy."

> *"He knows what he's talking about and keeps me awake during class. His classes are exciting. He brings in speakers and really gets involved in his teaching and includes everyone in the activities."* Cheryl, 10th grade

> *"I like teachers who enjoy what they're doing, who aren't there just to collect a paycheck."* Ellen, 9th grade

Type B Teachers

Before you walk into the school building each day, repeat, "I will not have more than one or two Type B teachers during my remaining years of school."

Type B teachers are *really* different. You got the word even before you started junior high: "Watch out for Miss . . . Mr. . . . Mrs. . . ." Type B teachers are the teachers who never get their names on the "Teacher of the Year" ballot.

Some of these teachers seem to be direct descendants of Albert Einstein, the mathematical genius. Type B teachers have "Einstein Minds"; they know their subjects but they can't seem to give out the information in a way that you can understand it!

Type B teachers have something else in common: When patience was handed out, they didn't get much of it. They have a low tolerance to noise. That's why they often invent wild methods for getting a noisy class quiet. Some Type B teachers probably wonder why they ever wanted to become teachers! Teaching isn't what they hoped it would be. So they punch a mental time clock each morning and do a disappearing act after school before anyone can find them to ask questions about homework assignments. They act like they're allergic to anyone between the ages of twelve and fifteen. You wonder if they wouldn't be happier selling insurance, or driving a bread truck or an eighteen-wheeler.

What can you do so you won't hate every minute of a class with a Type B teacher (who would probably be happier as a cook in a monastery, a dog catcher, or a trash collector)? You can come up with your own survival plan. Here are some ideas.

Plan A: Talk with your parents about your Type B teachers. Your parents probably had one or two of them in junior high, too. Ask your parents how they handled being in a Type B teacher's class. While you're talking, you may figure out that the only reason you don't like particular teachers is because you've heard other kids say *they* don't like them.

Plan B: Strain your eyes to see something good about your Type B teacher. If your best friend or group friends have the same class with this teacher, call a meeting and decide that each of you will try really hard to notice something good about that teacher. Once you find it, hang onto that good quality for the rest of the year; look for it every day.

Plan C: Give your Type B teacher genuine compliments. For example, "The bulletin board looks great!" "Thanks for helping me understand the assignment." "I like your outfit." You'll never know how much sincere compliments can help Type B teachers until you give them. Don't worry about being accused of trying to get in good with the teacher. There's nothing wrong with trying to encourage someone—even a Type B teacher! Check your motives to be sure you really mean and believe what you say.

Plan D: Talk to God about your Type B teachers. Tell him exactly how they make you feel and how you feel about them. You won't ever know how much this might help you *and* your teacher until you try it.

Plan E: If you feel comfortable doing it, ask one of your Type A teachers if they had any Type B teachers when they were in junior high and how they handled being in their classes.

How Girls Feel about Type B Teachers

"I can't respect teachers that can't control their classes." Christine, 10th grade

"She chews me out and it makes me feel weird." Cathy, 7th grade

"She has no patience." Aimee, 8th grade

"They think you're not trying hard enough, but you're trying your best." Alicia, 7th grade

"I disliked her because she couldn't get down to our level and then she'd pile the homework on us. She's too intelligent to be teaching junior high." Eileen, 9th grade

"She's the most boring person alive, but I also didn't like her because I didn't like math and the two sort of go together." Bonnie, 7th grade

"I can't understand why she doesn't like kids. They're fun!" Veronica, 8th grade

What You've Always Wanted to Know about Teachers But Were Afraid to Ask

Sometimes teachers seem to act like aliens from another planet. They do and say things that don't make sense and sometimes don't seem fair. This next section will give you answers to some of the questions you've probably been dying to ask since your first day in school!

Question #1: Why Do Teachers Give Homework?

Most teachers want students to know that homework isn't a form of punishment they dreamed up one day when they got mad at their class for being noisy. Some teachers even give time at the end of a class period to give students a running start on homework assignments. They do this so that if some of the students are still having trouble with the assignment, they'll be there to help them.

What Teachers Say about Homework

"Homework is necessary because we rarely remember what we hear only once." 9th grade teacher

"I give homework because fifty minutes isn't always enough time to discuss a new subject *and* to give my students individual assistance at the same time. If [students] are to learn the subject well it needs to be repeated. I don't feel that more than thirty minutes of homework should be assigned." 8th grade teacher

"Homework involves parents in their kids' education." 7th grade teacher

"Homework says, 'What should I have learned today?'" 8th grade teacher

"I use homework as a reinforcement to what students have learned in class. Sometimes not all new subjects are learned in class. Homework helps students understand what they didn't understand in class. . . . Here's the way I reduce homework assignments. I ask for oral and written reviews from the [previous day's] homework during the first ten minutes of class. The answers tell me if the lesson was understood. If the lesson isn't understood, I explain it again. My second method is offering points for doing homework in an acceptable way. When students know there is an extra reward, they don't mind homework quite as much." 9th grade teacher

"Homework is an 'evil necessity' of life." 10th grade teacher

It may be frustrating to you, but teachers have a legitimate reason for giving homework. When you complete your homework assignment you prove to yourself and to your teacher that you understand the subject and that you can do the work on your own. When you prove this year after year, you're preparing yourself for a great future.

Still think homework is a waste of time? Well, maybe these scenes will help you out.

Scene One: You put on your high school graduation gown and funny square hat and walk across the stage to get your signed high school diploma.

Scene Two: Four years later — if you choose to go to college — you put on another gown and funny hat, walk across another stage, and get a signed college diploma.

Scene Three: You walk into a new job and you succeed.

That's when you realize that all the homework you did on your own finally paid off. The work you produce tells your employer, "I did my 'homework.' I understand the job. I've proved I can do it on my own."

Whether you like it or not, homework will never be completely outlawed — but there *is* a simple formula to make sure you get less of it: passing fewer notes in class, plus throwing fewer paper wads and paper airplanes, plus daydreaming less, plus talking less to your friends, plus really listening while the teacher is explaining a new subject *equals* less schoolwork after hours.

Blessed is . . .

Blessed is the teacher who understands why homework must be given.

Blessed is the teacher who understands and can explain homework assignments.

Blessed is the teacher who gives extra time at the end of class periods to do homework.

Blessed is the student who *uses* the extra time to do the assigned homework.

Blessed are the parents who are smart enough to help their kids with homework.

Question #2: Why Do Teachers Yell?

Get this scene. You have been selected to be "Student Teacher for a Day." It's quite an honor—or so you think! You promise yourself you won't yell at your class because you hate it when "real" teachers yell.

You sweat it out preparing for the class. There's no way to know if the kids will like what you've prepared to teach.

You walk into your classroom the next day. You already know there are kids in the class who hate being there. Instead of sitting at their desks, the students are walking around, visiting with each other. A dusty eraser flies through the air; paper wads are being manufactured. One group is in a huddle and they're laughing. A girl is in a corner crying softly and her friend is trying to comfort her.

The bell rings. You try to get the class's attention. A few of the kids go to their desks and stare at you. Some of them start reading library books or comic books. Two girls keep talking about a certain guy who they think is a jerk.

You start teaching. The class gets noisier. You look at your watch. Forty-five minutes until the bell rings. You try to get the class's attention again. You use your patient, kind, soft voice. "Hey, if you all will listen I think you'll like what I have prepared to teach."

No response.

During the next five minutes you use a less patient, kind, soft voice. It looks like that isn't going to help either.

You have one choice left.

You *yell!*

Finally you have their attention. Now the class can hear you, and you can do what you were selected to do: teach.

Why do teachers yell? Most teachers say they yell because "kids don't listen."

Here's the way one teacher explains it: "When my class gets noisy, I say in my normal voice, 'Settle down.' If they don't settle down I say a little louder, 'I *need* your attention.' Some students might come back at me with some smart statement. They're the ones that get it full force. I don't do well with disrespect. I don't want the whole class to take my yelling personally, especially if they aren't involved in making noise.

"When students do what they're asked to do in a normal tone, teachers don't yell. When they don't respond, I have to change the volume of my voice so they can hear me."

How Other Teachers Feel about Yelling

"Frustration and stress can cause teachers to yell, especially when they have to repeat statements that deal with assignments." 8th grade teacher

"I have been accused of yelling. When students appear not to hear, I have the tendency to increase the volume of my voice so the whole class can understand. Students complain that they don't hear the instructions. Resisting the temptation to talk during class while the teacher is explaining the assignment would help." 7th grade teacher

"I never yell at my students. I feel yelling is a very ineffective means of classroom management. Instead I define the rules and limitations in my classroom and assign consequences for breaking rules or going beyond those limitations. If major rules are broken I try to handle those problems in private instead of in front of the whole class." 9th grade teacher

"I rarely get to the point that could be called yelling. If things are that bad I usually try to take a look at myself *first*. I should be smart enough to solve classroom problems without screaming at my students." 10th grade teacher

"I don't like to yell in my classroom. Students are surrounded by yelling all day; they don't need any more. If I have to yell there are two situations that cause it. Fighting between students can sometime only be stopped by yelling. Also, I may yell if a class activity is nearing completion and getting out of hand. This kind of yelling might take five seconds. Aside from that I hate to yell." 8th grade teacher

Teachers battle pollution: *noise* pollution. Sometimes a classroom has thirty or more voices going at the same time. Teachers have to jolt their classes with the kind of voices that will get some attention.

The easiest way to get rid of the noise problem would be to put gags on all the mouths that are moving without permission—but there's a better way. These Words give you some great advice for keeping teachers from yelling.

[There's] a time to be quiet; [and] a time to speak up. (Ecclesiastes 3:7)
A gentle answer turns away [a teacher's] wrath. . . . Gentle words cause life and health. (Proverbs 15:1, 4)

Want teachers who don't yell? Then listen in class and speak only when given permission. Try it during your next class. You'll like the results.

Question #3: How Do You Know a Teacher Cares about You?

Teachers wouldn't think of writing "I care about you" on an index card, then holding it in front of your face each day when you walk into the classroom. That's pretty dumb. But they *do* have their own special way of letting you know they care about you. Here are a few ways some teachers say they show their students they are interested in them and care about them.

They:
- tell you "Good morning." "You look great!" "Good game." "You can do it." "I'm here if you need me." "I know you did your best";
- tell you they'll come early or stay late to help you with an assignment or with a personal problem;
- let you know when they see your name or other family names in the newspaper or hear of one of your accomplishments;
- give you extra jobs to do, praise you when you improve in a subject, encourage you when you don't do well on a test, treat you with special respect, talk to you about after-school activities, compliment you for class input, listen to you, pray for you, cry for you.

If you have teachers who have done several of these things for you, your teachers are *normal!*

What Teachers Notice about You

Remember, teachers have eyes in back of their heads. They notice things about you that you wouldn't think they'd notice. Here are some of the things several teachers commented they notice.

Girls:
- travel in packs in the halls
- try to dress alike
- write notes in class
- talk about boys
- are bold around boys
- are shy around boys
- talk about other girls
- are sensitive to criticism
- are eager to please
- are self-conscious
- are enthusiastic
- are friendly

- are eager to share ideas
- love to talk on the phone
- have a sense of humor
- are creative
- giggle a lot
- can work independently
- genuinely care for others
- live in a world of sound (they can't stand silence)

If you have done several of these things, your teachers believe *you're* normal!

SIX

Secret
Feelings
about
Parents

> *Dear Diary,*
> *My parents bug me about being on the phone too long*
> *and going places with my friends. They just don't*
> *understand that I'm growing up and I want to do more*
> *things. I wish they wouldn't treat me like such a kid!*
>
> *Lindey*

Are you feeling differently about *your* parents lately? Maybe you don't want to hang around them as much as you did when you were younger, but they haven't caught on to that new feeling yet!

Several years ago you probably *wanted* to be around your parents. When they left you with a baby-sitter you squalled until they got home. You begged them to read you "one more" story at bedtime. You called them later to bring you a drink of water so you'd know they were still in the house.

You believed your parents could do anything. When you fell down and skinned your knees, your parents could make them feel better by kissing them. If you had a bad dream they could come into your room, hold you, tell you

113

not to be afraid, and you'd fall asleep again. You believed them when they said you should eat your vegetables because they were good for you.

You got used to having your parents, especially your mom, remind you to brush your teeth, comb your hair, wash your hands, do your homework, and a thousand other things. You didn't have to think much because your parents took turns working twelve-hour shifts reminding you to do what you were supposed to do.

Your parents are *still* giving you reminders, right? But they've probably added some new ones: "Get your hair out of your eyes," "Get your elbows off the table," "Stop smacking your lips," "Clean your room," "Stand up straight."

You wish your parents would understand that you *can* do some things without being told. You've felt this way since fifth and sixth grade — but the feeling is stronger now. You really want your parents to be part-time instead of full-time parents, but you aren't sure how to tell *them* that.

How Girls Feel about Their Parents

"They may want to help me but sometimes I just need to be alone. I spend a lot of time in my room. My parents think I'm trying to avoid them but that isn't true." Kim, 8th grade

"When I turned thirteen, they were still thinking I was ten years old and I resented that." Gerri, 9th grade

"They have a lot of faith in me and they let me use my own judgment. It makes me feel so good to be trusted by them but then I have to live up to their trust." Kari, 10th grade

"They treat me different now. More strict." Maggie, 7th grade

"Dad doesn't nag too much but Mom is always saying, 'Brush your teeth,' 'Make your bed.' I get used to it though." Kristin, 8th grade

"Some of the time they joke about sex, my period, friends,

etc. It really hurts. They can't understand how sensitive I am." Judy, 8th grade

"Mom and I are completely different people. She doesn't understand things I want and enjoy doing, and she can't understand why some things are important to me." Dawn, 9th grade

"When I was thirteen I wanted to go out with my friends instead of staying with my family all the time." Corey, 8th grade

"I like it when my parents are gone because I have the house to myself and I can sort out my thoughts." Krista, 8th grade

"I wish Mom would understand more about me and guys. I try to talk to her, but she just yells at me." Terri, 8th grade

"My mom and dad understand me. They're great." Lee, 9th grade

"I like it when my parents trust me and they do most of the time." Vicki, 7th grade

What is it with parents that make them do what they do? *Are* they really necessary to have around after elementary school?

What Do Parents Do?

Once you've made it to junior high, parents do a quick changing act. One girl said, "My parents have X-ray eyes now. They know where I am, what I'm doing, who I'm doing it with, and where I'm doing it. They always find out what I don't want anyone to know."

Another big change you may have noticed is that your parents have started taking a special interest in your room. They let you know when they aren't pleased with the way it looks, which is most of the time. You think your mother tries to come up with plans to make you feel guilty about the condition of your room. One really frustrating plan is the way she asks lots of questions:

"Honey, can you remember the last time you changed the sheets on your bed?"

"Doesn't it embarrass you when your friends come over and they see your room looking like this?"

"How can you find *anything* in this room?" (Usually the only time you *can't* find anything is after your mom has cleaned your room!)

"I tried to get into your room today. After I got in, I looked under your bed. Do you know there's something growing under there? Is it a science project you forgot to turn in?"

Why do parents want you to keep your room clean? Maybe they're afraid you might grow up to be a professional slob, and they would rather see you choose a profession that includes a salary. Or maybe they're trying to teach you responsibility.

Does it seem your parents are embarrassing you more now that you're in junior high? It probably would embarrass you to death if your dad did what he said he would do if your boyfriend ever came to the house. Then there's the way your dad dresses. You're sure your friends' dads wouldn't even think of wearing cowboy boots with sweats or a baseball cap with a suit. You don't have the nerve to tell your mom that it embarrasses you when she introduces you to her friends as "my baby," or when she hugs you in public. You're not sure what to say when your mom and dad try to use the same kind of words they *think* you and your friends use. (No one has told them kids don't say *groovy, hep,* or *cool* anymore.)

Shopping with your mom may not be as much fun as it used to be. When you were small she'd buy you a dress and tell you, "It looks darling on you." It's not the same now. You have your own likes and dislikes, but your mother doesn't agree with you. What you like, she *doesn't* like. The clothes *she* likes you wouldn't be caught dead in.

Do you know why you're feeling differently about your parents now? It isn't that you've stopped loving them. It's because *you and your parents have entered a new relationship with each other.* It's so new that neither of you knows quite how to handle it. You are pulling away from your parents . . . and *that's normal.*

You want your parents to treat you as an equal, to listen to you, and to respect your opinions. You didn't feel this way when you were small, but you do now and you want your parents to understand how much these things mean to you.

What Girls Wish Their Parents Knew about Them

"I wish my parents would treat me like a friend and not push too much responsibility on me. My life doesn't revolve around *dishes.*" Candy, 9th grade

"I wish they knew how I feel, how I think, how I like and hate, and how some things hurt." Ann, 8th grade

"I wish Mom and Dad would listen to me and not make fun or put down what I say. That irritates me when I really believe in something and they put it down." Gayle, 8th grade

"I wish they knew I have a lot more pressures than they think. They could be a lot more understanding when I get upset or want to be by myself. I wish they could understand my moods." Connie, 7th grade

"I want them to know I don't like my secrets told *and* I'm not a quitter." Julia, 9th grade

"I like it when my parents trust me and give me my own space." Jessica, 7th grade

"I like to dream and pretend." Leslie, 7th grade

"I wish they knew that I feel trapped. Mom says she's glad

I don't cuss and sleep around but I feel trapped and if I try to talk to her she just says, 'No, don't do it.' I wish we could talk about it." Barb, 10th grade

"I wish my parents knew that I'm reliable and that they can trust me *and* that I'm not a baby." Erin, 9th grade

"I want my parents to know that I don't and never have used drugs. I want them to know they can trust me and I don't need them to watch me like a hawk." Candy, 10th grade

"I need my parents to help me when I'm down. They do a lot for me, and that's why I need them." Pat, 8th grade

"I wish they'd go to events where I'm involved and watch me." Geneva, 7th grade

"I wish they knew that I'm a good person and I'm better than they think and I know what's right and wrong." Lucille, 10th grade

"I wish my parents knew I love them very much, but I'm not good at expressing myself." Gina, 9th grade

"I want them to know that I can be trusted and not have them think I'm wild and crazy. They always say that if you don't do this or that in life you'll be doomed! They pressure me a lot about school and parties and being gone a lot, but they really don't need to lecture me all the time. They aren't real possessive and I *do* know they care." Carla, 10th grade

"I need my independence. I can make grown-up decisions." Tess, 9th grade

"I don't want to do everything they want me to do anymore." Jaclyn, 8th grade

"I don't always like being their 'baby.' Sometimes I would like them to treat me more like a grown-up." Molly, 7th grade

"I like it when my parents trust me and let me make my own decisions but they don't always do it and that makes me mad." Michelle, 8th grade

"I'm not a child. I know what is right and wrong." Kaye, 8th grade

Maybe it would help you understand your feelings about your parents if you knew what your parents were *supposed* to do.

(It would help to ask your parents to read this section, too. If you have to, promise them you'll do the dishes every night for a week, make your bed every day for two weeks, or take out the trash for a month if they'll take the time to read this section. Believe me, you'll *both* be glad they did!)

What Parents Are Supposed To Do

Your mom and dad have some parental assignments straight from God. He tells them to make you beautiful inside — to "discipline" you (Proverbs 19:18), to teach you to "obey quickly and quietly" (1 Timothy 3:4), and to teach you to "love the Lord and not have a reputation for being wild or disobedient" (Titus 1:6).

While you're busy making yourself beautiful on the outside by choosing the clothes that are right for you, attacking pimples, and taking care of your fingernails and hair, your parents are doing what it takes to make you beautiful inside.

Helping to make you beautiful inside is a tough job. It includes encouraging you over and over to do your own work at school, to respect your teachers, to be considerate of older people, to say thank you, to be kind to little children (including your pesky bothers and sisters).

It means reminding you to do your homework, take out the trash, make your bed, clean the shower, put your dirty dishes in the sink or dishwasher, put your clothes away, and hold up your end of responsibilities around the house. Your parents don't have the choice of doing it differently. It goes with their job description. They clocked in to their job when you took your first breath and the job lasts at least eighteen years per child.

Some parents have read in the Bible that "children are a gift from God." So they do whatever they have to do to make their "gift" beautiful inside. Here's part of their job description:

The hardest part of raising children is teaching them to ride bicycles. A father can either run beside the bicycle or stand yelling directions while the child falls. A shaky child on a bicycle for the first time needs both support and freedom. The realization that this is what the child will always need can hit hard. (Sloan Wilson, The Man in the Grey Flannel Suit, Twenty Years Before and After; *New York: Arbor House, 1975)*

So parents are *supposed* to know when to be a part of your life and support you, and when to back off and give you freedom. This is harder for some parents than others, but they all can ask God to give them wisdom to know when to help their kids and when to back off. These Words can help parents know what they're *supposed* to do.

[Parents] teach [your daughter] to choose the right path [what's best for her] and when [she] is older [she] will remain upon it." (Proverbs 22:6)
Let each generation [parents] tell its children [you] what glorious things [God] does. (Psalm 145:4)
Don't keep on scolding and nagging your children, making them angry and resentful. Rather, bring them up with the loving discipline the Lord himself approves, with suggestions and godly advice. (Ephesians 6:4)
Let God train you, for he is doing what any loving [parent] does for his children. Whoever heard of a [daughter] who was never corrected? . . . Since we respect our [parents] here on earth, though they punish

us, should we not all the more cheerfully submit to God's training so that we can begin really to live? Our earthly [parents train] us for a few brief years, doing the best for us that they [know] how, but God's correction is always right and for our best. (Hebrews 12:7-10)

What Daughters Are Supposed To Do

You have two "Daughter Requirements." When you do them, you help keep your home from becoming a war zone for you and your parents. Requirement number one: Obey. "[Daughters] obey your parents; this is the right thing to do." Why? "Because God has placed them in authority over you" (Ephesians 6:1). And "young [woman], obey your father and your mother. Take to heart all of their advice" (Proverbs 6:20-21).

Requirement number two: Honor. "Honor [respect, value] your father and mother" (Ephesians 6:2). What do you do to honor your parents? You do what you can to let them know how you respect and value them for what they've done and are doing for you. Why? Because they've spent a lot of time taking care of you during all the stages of your life. They cared for you when you were a baby and when you were a preschooler. And they cared for you when you hit elementary school and junior high school.

Stage One: Infancy

During this stage, you threw baby food at your parents or spit it on them while they were feeding you, but they kept loving you anyway.

You cried a lot. When you cried, they rocked or bounced you or drove you all over town to stop your crying . . . but they kept loving you anyway.

Even after they registered the millionth diaper change they kept loving you. You left your teethmarks on the furniture and spilled milk in every room of the house, but they kept loving you anyway.

You threw temper tantrums in stores because they wouldn't let you (a) out of the grocery cart, (b) eat a whole bag of cookies, (c) have a new toy . . . *but they kept loving you anyway.*

Stage Two: Preschool

You tried out your new box of crayons and Mother's lipstick on the walls and floors of the house and they had to do a major paint job, but they kept loving you anyway.

They spent lots of time looking under beds, in closets, in the trash can, under the car seats, and behind furniture for your missing pacifier, favorite toy, or "blankie" . . . *but they kept loving you anyway.*

Stage Three: Elementary school

They kissed the hurts from your dirty knees and toes, but they didn't mind because they loved you.

They made sure you got all your immunity shots, then sat up with you through the nights when you were sick.

When they weren't cleaning up all the messes you made with scissors, glue, and glitter, they were showing you how to tie your shoes, ride your bike, tell time, and cross the street . . . *because they loved you.*

Stage Four: Junior High

Since you don't have your driver's license, your parents use lots of gas driving you to school, meetings, ball games, and parties. They don't complain too much because they love you.

They dream up new ways to drag you out of bed each morning so you won't miss school, because they love you.

They listen to you anytime, anywhere, because they love you.

They don't say much when they have to work around

curling irons, hair dryers, and brushes or stumble over dirty clothes, shoes, schoolbooks, and empty potato chip bags . . . because they love you.

They vote down a steady diet of pizza, hamburgers, fries, and Coke because they love you.

They have to tell you no sometimes . . . *because they love you.*

When you realize what your parents have done for you and what they're going to do for you, it helps you understand why God tells you to honor them. If that doesn't convince you, these Words might: "Honor your father and mother so that you may have a long, good life" (Exodus 20:12).

When you honor your parents, God tells you, "Well done," "Good job," "Way to go."

How Girls Can Honor Their Parents

God gave you a wonderful, creative mind. You can think of all kinds of ways to honor your parents. Most parents really do work hard at their jobs. Let them know that you respect them for working so hard. You *do* get some benefits from their hard work at their jobs in the form of clothes, food, and "motel accommodations."

When your mom fixes your favorite meals, keeps your clothes ready to wear, lets you have friends over, sits by you and listens to the good and bad parts of your day, let her know how much those things mean to you. When your dad knows enough about your school assignments to help you, let him know you couldn't do them without him.

If it's hard to tell your parents how much they mean to you, write them a note and leave it where they'll find it. It only takes five seconds to write, "I love you," "I appreciate you," "Thanks for putting up with me."

Even if your parents don't respond to your honoring them, you can go to bed at night knowing you did the best you could to let them know they are valuable people in your life.

It could be that no one has ever told them that they *are* important.

When It's Hard to Honor Your Parents

There are times it's hard to honor your parents — everyone knows that. You don't think they deserve to be honored. You believe they're asking too much of you. You have your own busy schedule but they want you to do all this other stuff, too. And you'll get grounded if you don't do what they say. It seems they really aren't interested in what's important to *you.*

Sometimes it feels like your days are filled with nagging, griping, arguing parents. You can't do anything right. You never quite please your parents with the way you clean your room, the grades you make, the friends you choose. With all this going on, there's no way you'd nominate your parents for the "Honored Parent Award."

Some parents have a hard time expressing what they feel for their children. I know a mother who, as far as I know, has never hugged her children. The way she talks about them, you get the idea that her kids have never done anything right, that they've always made wrong choices.

Maybe your parents are like that. Maybe it would help you to try to understand why your parents act the way they do. Try talking to or writing to your grandparents and ask them to tell you about your parents when they were kids. Hearing these facts might help you understand why your parents treat you and talk to you the way they do. Then maybe you could *consider* honoring them the way God tells you to. You may even want to ask God to *help* you to honor your parents.

Sometimes things happen that seem so awful that they make it almost impossible for kids to honor their parents. One of those things is when parents divorce.

When Parents Divorce

If your parents get divorced, the requirement to "honor your father and mother" might get lost in all the hurt, loneliness, and anger you feel.

My parents never divorced, but I knew some kids whose parents did. I tried to imagine how I would have felt if my parents had divorced. I thought I'd be mad at them for letting it happen and for breaking up our family. I would've been scared because I wouldn't have known which parent to choose to live with because I loved both of them.

I think I would have had all kinds of questions to ask them: "When and why did you stop loving each other?" "Why can't we all live together?" "Why can't you work out what's wrong between you?" "What's going to happen to us now?"

One of my friends told me that when her parents divorced, they told her they had decided to wait to get their divorce until after she went to college. They thought it wouldn't hurt her as much then. She said, "They were wrong! I never knew anything could hurt so much."

If your parents are divorced, or if you've heard them talking about getting a divorce, it may be hard for you to tell them how you're feeling about it. Your feelings get mixed up; you feel anger, sadness, loneliness, hopelessness, embarrassment, fear, and lots of other feelings that show up when parents leave each other.

One thing's for sure, your parents didn't schedule a divorce when they got married. It was probably the farthest thing from their minds! Sometime, though, after they were married, they started having problems and they didn't know how to work them out. So they decided it would be best for them and for you if they didn't live together any longer.

God had a perfect plan for marriage: "At the beginning God created man and woman . . . [and the] man should leave his father and mother, and be forever united to his wife. The two shall become one—no longer two, but one! And no man may divorce what God has joined together" (Matthew 19:4-6).

God planned that a man and a woman would notice each other out of thousands of other men and women. The man would get up his nerve to ask the woman for a date. She would accept. Later, they'd fall in love, get married, and stay together forever. It was a wonderful plan.

Then sin was allowed in and it invaded God's perfect plan for marriage. The minute sin showed up, things went wrong. One of the first married couples started having problems and they didn't want to be married any longer. All the husband had to do was say to his wife, "I divorce you," and that ended their marriage. Pretty soon so many couples were getting divorces that a man named Moses had to make some rules.

This is what Moses came up with: "If a man doesn't like something about his wife, he may write a letter stating that he has divorced her, give her the letter, and send her away" (Deuteronomy 24:1). Moses' rule permitted divorce, but "it was not what God had originally intended" (Matthew 19:8).

God's perfect plans were that a man and woman would get married and stay married forever. But many plans don't *stay* perfect because *people* aren't perfect, and they make mistakes. Divorce is one of the mistakes married couples make.

 ### How Girls Feel about Their Parents' Divorce
"It's the worst thing that ever happened in my life. We were all so close. I never thought this would happen. It's really

hard. I feel abandoned. There's nothing in the world that will ever feel so bad." Ellen, 7th grade

"I wish they would have divorced when I was real little so it wouldn't hurt so bad." Sandi, 9th grade

"I felt sad when my parents divorced because I loved both of them very much. It has changed my life. My mom cries all the time and that makes me feel very sad." Ronnie, 8th grade

"I'm glad my parents got a divorce because they went the last six years of their marriage with no feelings toward each other." Kathy, 9th grade

"Soon I'll be thirteen and have to choose who I want to live with. It's going to be a hard decision because I love both of my parents the same. It has affected me in many ways. I'm doing really bad in school. It makes Mom upset, but she understands." Colleen, 7th grade

"I think it's the worst thing that's ever happened to me. It happened when I was nine. Sometimes I still cry at night thinking about all the good times we had with both of my parents when they were together." Carol, 7th grade

"I don't think anyone understands how much it hurts. It's not fair! Where's my say in the divorce?" Marie, 8th grade

"I wish my parents could understand that all I want is a real family. My mom and dad are split up and it hurts." Anita, 9th grade

"I've wondered if my parents divorced because of me. What did I do wrong?" Nancy, 7th grade

Hear This!

If your parents are divorced, have you ever thought it was your fault that they got the divorce? Hear this! If you went to a hundred professional counselors they would tell you these same things.

Your parents' divorce is their problem. *You are not responsible* for their problems.

127

If your parents fight over you, *you are not responsible* for their fighting.

You are not responsible for trying to get your parents back together.

You are not responsible for deciding which parent gets custody of you.

You *are* responsible for something, though. You are responsible for being honest about what you are feeling, and for letting yourself have those feelings. You will probably grieve over your parents' divorce, and that's OK. You must *let yourself grieve* the way you feel it's best and most healthy for you.

You probably feel very alone, like no one really understands how you feel. I want you to know that God understands. You may even have heard this before, but it's really true. God is the only one who knows how badly your parents' divorce has hurt you. You may hurt for a long time, but here are some special Words that can help you when you don't think anyone else can help make your hurt go away.

> *God is [your] refuge and strength, a tested help in times of trouble. (Psalm 46:1)*
> *He does not ignore the prayers of [people] in trouble when they call to him for help. (Psalm 9:12)*
> *Give your burdens to the Lord. He will carry them. (Psalm 55:22)*
> *Though I am surrounded by troubles [and the problems and hurts of my parents' divorce] you [God] will bring me safely through them. (Psalm 138:7, emphasis added)*

What You Must Do

There are several things you can do to help yourself get through what is happening. Ask your parents to tell you *why* they're getting a divorce. Let one of your Type A teachers know that your parents are divorcing, since it may affect your class work.

Don't hurt alone. Talk to a caring adult who will listen.

If you're having trouble with your feelings about the divorce, tell your parents that you may need help from a professional counselor. Ask the counselor for some suggestions to help you work through your feelings.

Peace Talks

Everyone in your family stays busy, right? The only way your parents know you're still living at home is that they see your schoolbooks on the kitchen table, your dirty clothes piled by the clothes hamper, or a shoe and sock that have been resting in the middle of the living room for two weeks.

The only way you know your parents haven't moved and left you behind is that you smell food cooking in the kitchen, you see *their* dirty clothes piled up by *your* dirty clothes, and their bed is unmade . . . like yours!

As busy as your family gets, you need to talk together. One great way for your family to touch base with each other at least once a week is with some "Peace Talks."

Peace Talks are times when you get together with your family at a planned time . . . and talk. Some of your Peace Talks will involve discussing problems. Most of the time these talks will just help you stay acquainted with each other and aware of what's going on in each other's lives.

One thing you may discover during your Peace Talks is that parents really aren't boring and a pain when you know some facts about them. The things you learn may even help you understand why your parents say and do strange things.

Some of the best places to meet for Peace Talks are at the meal table, while you're scrunched up in the car going someplace together, or when a miracle occurs and *all* of you are sitting in the same room at the same time.

Peace Talk Starters

Try to have a Peace Talk with your parents at least once a week. Peace Talks can be done anytime you're together with one or both of your parents. Here are some ideas you might use at different Peace Talks.

1. Everyone take a turn to tell one other person what they appreciate about him or her.

2. Each person say three things he or she believes are true about him or herself. Then say three things you believe are true about the other family members. (These are to be positive statements.)

3. Everyone finish the following sentences:

• "Remember when we . . . " (Example: Remember when we all went sleigh riding together and we got so cold that we thought our hands and feet would fall off before we got home? Mom made a big pot of hot chocolate while we were taking off our wet clothes. We sat around talking, drinking and thawing out. It was great!)

• "I feel . . . about myself." Each person can tell the others whether or not he or she wants anyone to respond. Even if no response is made, this sentence lets the other family members know how each person is feeling. Everyone must respect that feeling.

• "I've never . . ." Each person should tell something he or she has never done. Maybe your family will decide to do some of the things.

• "If I could change one thing about our family it would be . . ."

4. Ask the following questions.

You ask your parents:

• "When you were small, what did you want to be when you grew up and why did you want to be that?"

• "What's the worst grade you ever got in school and how did your parents react to the grade?" (This one might help you find out something brand new about your parents' school years.)

Your parents ask you:

● "If you could choose any profession you wanted, what would it be? Why?"

Ask each member of the family:

● "What is the best family vacation you've had? Why was it the best?"

● "What have you gotten teased about? How did it make you feel? How did you react to the teasers?"

● "What kinds of pressure do you get from other people?" (You may be surprised to find the kinds of pressures your parents feel.)

● "What was the funniest thing that ever happened to you, that almost had you rolling on the floor?"

● "What's something that really bothers you? If you had the power to change it, how would you do it?"

● "Who has been your favorite teacher? What made that one teacher special?"

Try making up some of your own Peace Talk questions. The nice thing about Peace Talks is that as you get used to talking to each other, it will become easier to talk about and handle problems when they come up.

Handling Problems at Peace Talks

Here are two types of problems that might come up with your parents and some suggestions for how to deal with them in a Peace Talk.

Problem #1: Some family members think too much is being expected of them around the house.

Appoint a secretary. Put the name of each family member across the top of a piece of paper. Have each person tell what his or her responsibilities are around the house. The secretary records each job mentioned under the appropriate name.

If the list shows that certain members have more jobs than others, *everyone* should help make a new list and shift some of the responsibilities so the list will be more balanced.

Problem #2: You need to talk with your parents about a rule you think is unfair.

Rules can be a real pain. For example: "No talking on the phone after 8:00," "One hour of TV each night during the school year," "You can't do anything else until your homework is finished," "Bedtime is 10:00."

For this problem, try trading places. You be the parent, your parents will be you. Talk about the rule from each other's point of view. As you talk from these positions, one of four things may happen: (1) the rule will stay the same, (2) the rule will be rewritten, (3) the rule will be dropped, or (4) a compromise will be made between you and your parents.

If you can, put some humor into the role play. It takes some of the pressure and tension away from disagreements.

Another way to handle this particular problem is to have your parents give reasons why a certain rule is necessary, then you give reasons why you feel the rule *isn't* necessary. Discuss your reasons, then decide together if the rule *is* necessary or if it needs revising.

If it's difficult for you to talk to your parents, write what you'd like to say to them. Ask them in the note to think about what you've written before they talk with you about it. This gives both of you some thinking time.

Any time there's more than one person living in the same house, it's important for everyone to know how each person is feeling. No one can smell or taste a need, they have to hear it. That's why it's so important to have family Peace Talks. These Words tell you why:

> *Try to live in peace with everyone; work hard at it. For the eyes of the Lord are intently watching all who live good lives. (Psalm 34:14-15)*
>
> *I will try to walk a blameless path, but how I need [God's] help, especially in my own home, where I long to act as I should. (Psalm 101:2, emphasis added)*

How Girls Feel about Talking to Their Parents

"My parents are very understanding and I don't really think they should change anything except I wish we could talk more." Darcy, 8th grade

"I wish my parents would listen to my side and try to understand that things are different than they used to be when I was small." Deane, 9th grade

"I like it when my parents sit down and take the time to talk to me. My mom comes into my room and talks to me and we talk while we listen to the radio. I love the feeling it gives me." Sue, 7th grade

"I want to talk to my parents more openly." Edee, 8th grade

"I like it when my parents talk to me as an adult and not as a child, or when they tell me I'm a good person and tell me they love me . . . mistakes and all." Becky, 9th grade

"I wish I could talk to Mom about private stuff, like sex and stuff." Deborah, 8th grade

"I wish my parents would be home more and that we could talk out some things." Tammi, 7th grade

Two Good Reasons Why You Have Parents

Reason #1: You can blame your parents for the way you look.

It's pretty obvious that you inherited the same kind of

nose that's hooked to your mom's or dad's face. Whether you like your hair color or not, you inherited it from one of your parents.

Maybe you've never liked the toes that are attached to your feet and you have terminally white skin. When you look at your mom's or dad's feet or skin, you know where you got yours. Whatever feelings you have about your shape and looks, you can blame (or thank) dear old Mom and Dad for it all.

Reason #2: Parents teach their kids how to sort dirty clothes.

The week after Beth left for college, I wrote her a letter. I wanted to explain what I had been trying to get across to her for seventeen years.

Dear Beth,

Remember how I taught you to sort dirty clothes when it was time to do the weekly washing? I showed you how to put the white clothes in one pile, the towels in another pile, and the colored clothes in another pile.

You thought that was a dumb thing to teach you, until you picked up a piece of clothing that had dark and light colors in it and some of the other clothes weren't really white and some weren't really dark.

Since you didn't know which pile to put the clothes in, you asked me so the white clothes wouldn't come out of the washer permanently pink or grey and the dark clothes wouldn't have towel fuzz hanging on them.

While you were living with us, there were times when you weren't sure if certain things belonged in your life. You weren't sure about making certain decisions. Several times you'd ask Dad or me and we'd tell you what we thought. We gave you the best advice we knew to give and as hard as it was for us to do, we had to let you make the final decision.

Well, I've said it. Hope it helps you to know we love you, we want the best for you, and we'll be praying for you as you "sort clothes" without us.

Love,
Mom

Even if you think your parents invented the wheel, lived in trees or caves, saw dinosaurs roaming the earth, or have the word *old-fashioned* tattooed across their foreheads, they *do* know whether or not certain things should be a part of your life. It's part of their job of making you beautiful inside.

Parents don't get their thrills by disappointing you. It's hard for them to say no when you're on your knees, pulling on their clothes, begging, screaming or crying, trying to convince them that "Everybody's going to the party but me," "I'm the only one who doesn't have my own phone," "Everyone else's parents let their kids skip school sometimes," "*Their* parents don't stick around when they have a party at their house," "I'm the only girl at school who doesn't get to wear makeup."

When your parents don't give in and say yes, try hard to remember their special assignment from God. It's tough. Their assignment would be easier if you had been born with a set of instructions stamped on your bottom, but you weren't. So 95 percent of all POWs (Parents of the World) do the best they know how without instructions. They didn't even have a class to take to help them understand how you'd change when you got to junior high. Maybe that's why they make mistakes sometimes.

While you're checking into the possibility of putting your parents up for adoption or on the auction block, or buying them a one-way ticket to _____ (you choose the destination), repeat slowly ten times *or* until you believe it, "My parents *are* doing the best they know how."

Here's an assignment for you and your parents. Do this once a day for one month. If things change around your house after the month is up, you may decide to keep it up until you start receiving your social security checks.

1. Give each other a compliment once a day. For example:
Parent: "Hey, daughter, thanks for doing the dishes."
Daughter: "Hey, parent, thanks for not dirtying so many dishes so I could get them washed in less than two hours."

2. Hug each other once a day. (Did you and your parents think hugging went out of style with the Civil War? Try to remember how good hugging felt when you were little. It *still* feels good. Give it a try. It's painless.)

3. Tell each other, "I love you" once a day. If this is too difficult, write "I love you" on an index card and flash it in each other's face once a day.

4. Pray for each other once a day. Thank God for something special you see in each other. For example:
Daughter: "God, thank you that my parents are here when I need them."
Parent: "God, thank you for making our daughter beautiful inside."

What a way to *honor* each other!

What Parents Think about Their Daughters

"The way she feels about herself is causing her problems. [She's so worried about] whether she's 'pretty' or 'ugly', whether she's 'dumb' or 'smart'."

"She worries about skin problems, math, and has problems with her older brother."

"She is very interested in wearing the 'right' clothing and having her hair 'just right.' She talks a lot on the phone."

"She has frequent mood swings."

"She's a daydreamer."

"She's more open and sensitive to other people and their needs."

"My daughter is becoming a unique individual, and she's beginning to make some good decisions on her own."

"She's becoming more like a friend to me."

What Parents Wish Their Daughters Knew about Them

"Parents can't be mind readers. I try to tell my kids to tell me when they have a problem with a teacher or a friend, or any other thing that's bothering them."

"Kids need to know that parents are human and many times [parents] aren't having their needs and desires met, either."

"I want to feel that I can be honest about my feelings and emotions when I'm around my daughter. I don't want to hide my anger, hurt, etc., and I want to explain *why* I'm feeling the way I am when necessary."

"When both parents are working, the parents have times when they need privacy and time alone as well as spending time as a family."

"If a junior high daughter could understand that parents are human, too, and that they also make mistakes and have problems to deal with, it would be easier for her to understand her parents."

P.S.

I Forgot
To Tell
You about
Crawdads!

You probably think it's strange to end a book about girls with a story about crawdads. But something happens to crawdads that makes me think of what's happening to you during junior high. I'll tell you about crawdads, then I'll explain what and why you need to know about these ugly little creatures!

There are two unusual and interesting facts about adult crawdads. Their skeletal system is on the outside of their bodies *and* they only take time out for a few weeks each year to grow approximately one inch.

As long as a crawdad is locked into the size of its old shell it can't grow, but it has a great plan to get the shell off so it can grow.

She (this crawdad will be a "she" since this is a book for girls) starts getting rid of her old shell by rubbing her tiny legs together. Then she begins wiggling each leg. Next, she flips over on her back and begins to move her tail up and down. The old shell starts getting loose.

She gives one big push and the part of the shell around her head pops loose, except for the part around her mouth. She works slowly to loosen that part because she could

DEAR DIARY . . .

lose an eye or damage her antennas if she isn't careful.

After that part of the shell is loose, she yanks her legs out of the shell. Even if she's careful, she may break off one of her legs. She gives one more powerful, final push and the shell pops off. Without her shell, her soft body looks like a piece of wet paper. Then she rests a while because it has taken lots of energy to get the shell off.

After resting, she's ready to eat. Her first meal is usually the old shell. It has some minerals in it that will help her grow her new shell.

In a few weeks her body grows an inch before the new shell hardens. Now she's locked into her new size for another year. When the next year rolls around, she starts the growing process all over again.

So what does this story have to do with you? Every time *you* have a new experience, you grow a new "shell." Some of your experiences are painful, some aren't.

The painful experiences come when:

- Your best friend doesn't want to be your best friend anymore,
- Someone tells something about you that isn't true,
- Your boyfriend finally tells you that he only likes you as a "friend,"
- You lose a school election,
- You barely miss getting on the honor roll or getting an "A" you worked so hard to get,
- Your Type B teacher doesn't understand your hurts,
- Your parents make a mistake,
- *You* make a mistake!

Squeezed in between the painful experiences are the ones you'd like to have happen *all* the time:

- A best friend comes along just when you need her most,
- A guy falls for your plan to get him to notice you,
- You win an election at school,

140

- You pass the class you thought you were going to fail,
- A Type A teacher says you've got "great potential,"
- Your parents give you more freedom and say, "We trust you!"
- You can laugh at yourself for doing and saying dumb things,
- Someone sends you flowers,
- You look at yourself in a full-length mirror and admit that you like what you see,
- You really believe God designed you special,
- You admit to yourself that you're *normal!*

It may not seem to make sense, but it takes both kinds of experiences to grow new shells. A crawdad knows she has to get rid of her old shell if she's going to get a new one, but she also knows that some pain will be involved in getting it.

One girl wrote on her questionnaire: "Mom and Dad aren't going to be able to keep me as their 'baby' all my life. They *try* to tell me not to do certain things so I won't get hurt, but we have to get hurt sometimes to learn from our problems and mistakes." I wish I could meet this girl. She grew a new shell when she realized that problems and mistakes and painful parts of growing have to be mixed in with all the good stuff to help her grow more beautiful inside.

Even before I started writing this book, I did everything I could to learn more about the feelings *and* needs of junior high girls. I stood in the halls of their schools, sat in their classrooms, called them on the phone, watched them pass notes and giggle during church worship services, observed how they got along with their moms while they were shopping together, watched them laughing and having great times with their friends, and noticed how they put their "flirt plans" into action. After several weeks, I was ready to write.

I spent many hours writing this book with you in mind. Sometimes I'd stop writing and try to imagine what you looked like, what you were doing, and how you were feeling about all the changes that were going on in your life. I lay in bed at night and wondered if you were going through some painful experiences or if you were having days with all the good stuff happening.

I prayed that each subject I included, each word I chose to put on paper, would help you discover that beautiful young woman inside you. I wanted you to know that following God's plan for you will help you make a big impact on the world.

If no one has told you in the last twenty-four hours, I want to tell you now that the world *is* a better place because you're here—*and* you're doing great!

Don't forget to write me!

Love,
Pat

Getting in the Last Words

"O Lord . . . you created my inmost being; you knit me together in my mother's womb. I praise you because I am fearfully and wonderfully made" (Psalm 139:1, 13-14, NIV).